*"I want to understand the world from
to know what you know in the way th... ,
understand the meaning of your experience, to walk in your
shoes, to feel things as you feel them, to explain things as you
explain them. Will you become my teacher and help me
understand?"*

(Spradley, 1979)

Do m'athair agus mo mháthair,
Clíodhna

Contents

Introduction: 11

Chapter 1: 13

    The Specialist Palliative Care Unit 15

Chapter 2: 19

    What is Qualitative Research? 19

    How Qualitative Research applies to Health Care Research 19

    Narrative medicine and Qualitative Research 20

    Qualitative Research in Palliative Medicine 21

    Qualitative versus Quantitative research 23

    Clinical discourse and how its methods parallel with Qualitative Research 27

    Qualitative Research in Health Science Research 29

    Methods used in Qualitative Research: Sampling Methods 31

    Observation in Qualitative Research 33

    Bias in Qualitative Research 34

    Validity in Qualitative Research 35

    (i) Triangulation 35

    (ii) Reflexivity 36

    How well does the analysis explain why people behave in the way they do? 36

    How comprehensible would the explanation of the conclusions of the study be to a thoughtful participant in the setting? 37

    How well does the explanation cohere with what we already know? 37

    Validation by Respondents 37

    Attention to negative cases 38

    Interviewing in Qualitative research 38

    Structured interviewing 39

Field-notes and researcher diary 44
Use of Computers in Qualitative Research......................................45
Transferability 46
Data Analysis in Qualitative Research 46
Chapter 3: 55
Traditions of death and dying in Ireland 56
Death and Dying in the modern-day setting...................................57
The Moment of Death..59
Defining the moment of death in this study 59
A 'Good Death'..60
Some Global Statistics relating to the Place of Death 65
The Medicalization or Institutionalisation of Dying 70
Research..74
Chapter 4. 79
Defining "Ethics" 79
Ethics in Palliative Medicine...79
Ethics in Qualitative Research...80
After-death interviews with relatives in this study 81
Chapter 5: 89
An Epiphany 93
Soul Pain 95
Education 97
Attitudes to Spirituality and Ritual in this study on the Moment of Death...99
Chapter 6: 101
Review 101
Method..105

Findings 119
The Moment of Death.. 119
Awareness of life beyond death.. 124
Vigil. 125
Ritual and Prayer 126
The Qualities of Staff 127
The Specialist Palliative Care Unit.. 128
Love and respect shown for the dead body 133
Humour... 134

Chapter 7: 135
Field-Notes: Introduction 135
Some Conclusions 141
Study Limitations: Selection of participants 142
Setting confined to one Specialist Palliative Care Unit........................ 144
Potential Interview Bias... 144
Bias in Data analysis.. 145
This Study: Research Strengths 147
Of benefit to the participants 147
Provide incentives for future research 147
Further education at undergraduate and postgraduate levels............... 148
Incentives for future research 154
Further Conclusions... 155

Appendices 165
Appendix 8.1 165
Appendix 8.2 165
Appendix 8.3 165
Appendix 8.4 166

Appendix 8.5 167
(Select) References 168
About The Authors..174

Introduction:

Mícheál Ó hAodha

School of Languages, Cultures and Communications
University of Limerick, Limerick. Ireland

The making and unmaking of myths is always new. This volume explores the tradition of death in Irish culture but does so from a new and unique perspective – how death applies to the individual in Ireland, how the narrative of death is "constructed"; how Irish attitudes to death as presented in this study are an amalgam of a very "old" tradition (incorporating specific traditional spiritual practices as relating to Christianity and Catholicism) – a tradition that is a conversation between the living world and the threshold of death – i.e. the present-day palliative and caring tradition, as associated with dying and the moment of death itself.

This volume explores the "divided" postcolonial mind that is characteristic of Ireland as a country and of the Irish as a people. It is a volume that is as much to do with identity as it is to do with spirituality, attachment to place and the rituals as associated with death and dying in a modern/postmodern Irish setting.

From the foundational myth of Cú Chulainn to the "Dead" or "living dead" of Joyce or the dark laughter of Beckett and Ó Cadhain, the historical and deeply traditional association of the Irish with death and dying has remained constant and unwavering. It is a leitmotif that pervades the cultural sphere to this very day with many public commentators now associating the decline and depopulation of rural Ireland and the return of wide-scale emigration as a form of death.

By exploring the range of older and emergent discourses that articulate death and dying in present-day Ireland, unusually in many ways, we witness the unbroken transmission of long established values and ritual actions focussed on death, dying and how the dying person and their family cope with this most definitive of realities.

Despite its traditional significance, the moment of death which is the focus of this study has largely remained unexplored in a hospice setting. While we can never hear the stories of the dead, it is possible for us to listen to the stories of those who have witnessed dying, particularly when these reflections and perspectives come from relatives who cared deeply for the individual who was dying. One aspect of death which is common to all cultures is the careful observation and recollection of every detail as it relates to the dying person. People later recount every word and action on the part of the dying person their role in accompanying them on the journey that is death, and the subsequent bearing witness to its nature. A study such as this makes it possible to reclaim notions of identity, continuity and tradition while simultaneously considering the endurance and primacy of the symbolism associated with death, dying and the funerary code in modern Irish culture. This volume makes it possible to view these important questions in a new light.

Chapter 1:
"The Moment of Death":
Emotional and Spiritual
Significance in the Irish Context

The All- Ireland Institute for Hospice and Palliative Care (HRB, 2007) have stated that across Europe, end of life care is on the agenda as never before. Although concentration is in countries in the west, there is growing evidence that the provision of hospice and palliative care is attracting the interests of policy makers and funding bodies as well as health and social care professionals, patients, families and the wider public. Ireland in particular has a rich culture and tradition of hospice and care of the dying, passed down to us from our ancestors. (Donnelly 1999 (a)).

A World Health Organisation report however (Fleck, 2004), has found in certain parts of Europe palliative care services are severely limited. In poorer countries of the world, palliative care is still underdeveloped. The report (Fleck, 2004) calls on all health policy makers to urgently make palliative care a core part of their health care services.

In 1990, the World Health Organisation stated that palliative medicine "affirms life and regards dying as a normal process, neither fosters nor postpones death, provides relief from pain, integrates the spiritual and psychological aspects of care, offers help to patients to live as actively as possible until death and offers a support system to help families cope during the patient's illness and in their bereavement." Highly technical investigations and treatment are utilized only when their benefits outweigh any potential burden to the dying patient (Donnelly, 1995). Palliative medicine itself represents a compassionate response to the unrelieved suffering of the dying and involves a commitment to improving clinical skills and so, the conditions where healing can occur (Kearney, 1992). Palliative medicine is now recognized as a distinct medical speciality, firstly by the Royal College of Physicians,

London, in 1987 (Donnelly, 1995) and by the Royal College of Physicians of Ireland in 1995 (RCPI, 2008).

The term "palliative care" was first proposed in 1974 by a leading Canadian surgeon Balfour Mount (Donnelly, 2008). The word palliative is derived from the word "palliare", to cloak. The cloak, mantle or shroud had a significance in the philosophy of the people in our past who cared for the dying where the dead body was cloaked in a shroud or mantle and to whom we as palliative care professionals have inherited consciously or unconsciously (Donnelly, 1999, (b)). The rise of palliative care has been one response to calls for greater dignity at the end of life. It has encouraged medicine to be gentler in its acceptance of death. (Clark, 2002). The principles of palliative medicine apply wherever people suffer in dying and are appropriate and applicable in the practice of all doctors, regardless of their speciality (Donnelly, 1995). The connections between the past and present in the care of the dying contain a powerful, symbolic message. It suggests that modern hospices are rooted in deep and ancient traditions of compassionate care that go back to earliest civilizations. However it is inaccurate to draw too close a parallel between 'hospices' in early times and those in the twentieth and twenty first centuries (HHP, 2008). In earlier times those taken care of were the poorest of the poor, with a wide range of diseases and were cared for over longer periods of time. In later times the diseases were mainly malignancies and people were cared for closer to death. In the nineteenth century both the bereaved and the medical establishment noted the first signs of death as a medical failure. The dying were no longer welcome in hospital, so women such as Jeanne Garnier, widowed and bereaved, with others, formed L' Association des Dames du Calvaire in Lyons, France. They opened a home for the dying characterized by "a respectful familiarity, an attitude of prayer and calm in the face of death" (Clark, 2000). Palliative care services exist to-day in Paris and New York as a result of this work.

In Ireland, Mary Aikenhead, born in 1787, was later to found and become Superior to the Order of the Sisters of Charity. Three of the sisters went to Paris to learn of the work of the L'hôspital de Notre

Dame de la Pitié and later returned to open St Vincent's Hospital in Dublin in 1834. A further hospice Our Lady's hospice, Harold's Cross opened in 1879. The Sisters of Charity opened other hospices around the world in Australia, England and Scotland. (HHP, 2008). Mother Mary Aikenhead had a holistic vision for hospice care expressed in the mission statement of Our Lady's hospice, Harold's Cross:

"Strives through a team approach in an atmosphere of loving care to promote wholeness of body, mind and spirit". (OLH, 2009)

Dame Cicely Saunders founded St Christopher's Hospice in London in 1967. Its success was huge and was an inspiration to other hospices around the world. It became the example of a "modern" hospice and three principles of clinical care, education and research (Saunders, 1964). During the 1950's concerns about improving care at the end of life began to emerge on both sides of the Atlantic. A shift took place in the literature as regards care of the dying. By the early 1960's leading articles in the Lancet and the British Medical Journal were drawing on evidence to suggest ways in which care of the dying could be promoted. A view of dying began to emerge that sought to foster concepts of dignity and of meaning along with a new openness about the condition of the dying patient (Clark, 2002). Palliative care and hospice programs originally addressed the needs of dying patients with tuberculosis or cancer. Since then programs have developed assisting patients with AIDs, motor-neurone disease and any other disorders characterized by constantly changing physical symptoms, increased risk of psychosocial distress and relatively short period of final illness (Donnelly, 1995).

The Specialist Palliative Care Unit
This study on the moment of death takes place in a Specialist Palliative Care Unit (SPCU) in the South-West region of Ireland. At the time of this qualitative study the Palliative Medicine Department provided 20 beds, now increased to 30 beds covering a maximum radius of 25 miles throughout the whole mid-west region. Palliative homecare services with 15 clinical nurse specialists served the

surrounding areas. Though patients with cancer are predominantly admitted to SPCU, patients with other end-stage illness are increasingly being admitted. There were a total of 618 admissions to the SPCU during this study between Jan 2001- Jan 2003. The number of deaths during the same period were 350.

Palliative care extends from hospice care to the acute hospital setting to home care in the community and day-care. At present, in Ireland, the initiative of Hospice Friendly Hospitals programme is underway (IHF, 2008), facilitating the provision of palliative care as a fundamental service in all acute hospitals. Its three key objectives include:

1. Developing standards around end-of-life issues in hospitals
2. Developing the capacity of hospitals to introduce and implement these standards
3. To change the culture of hospitals regarding end-of-life issues.

The Health Services Executive (HSE) in Ireland have published a five year developmental framework from 2009-2013 (HSE, 2009) which addresses deficits in the palliative care service provision in the four HSE regions Ireland. The report states that more than 6,000 people use the hospices in Ireland every year and because of Irelands ageing population up to 13,000 will use hospice services by 2016. The document states that 9 new hospices need to be built in Ireland, increasing hospice beds from the present 153 to 356. There is considerable variation in the availability of palliative care services throughout the country with no inpatient hospice services in some areas (HSE, 2009). Alhough the speciality that is palliative care is becoming more well-known in Ireland, there is still a great need for support and funding for the ongoing development of its services in Ireland. Fig 1.2 demonstrates the overall timescale and outline of this Qualitative Enquiry into the Moment of Death in a Specialist Palliative Care Unit.

Fig 1.2
Study Design

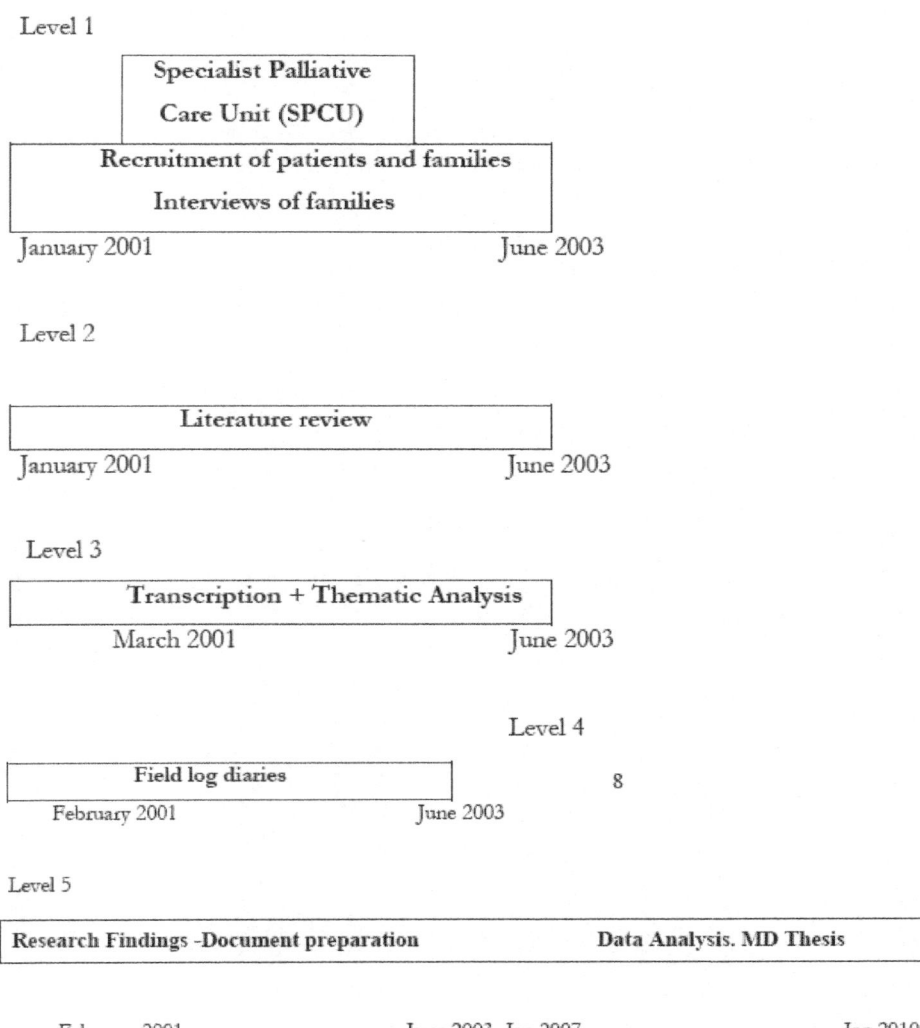

Chapter 2:

"A Good Death":
Irish Palliative Medicine, Tradition and the Qualitative Research Approach

Qualitative Research

What is Qualitative Research?
Qualitative methods have their roots in social anthropology which was founded on studies in which an understanding of the customs and behaviour of people from remote lands was obtained by researchers who spent time living in those societies, learning their languages, participating while observing. In essence, qualitative research involves, watching, joining in and talking with the group being studied. Bradley (1997) defines qualitative research methods as methods of collection, analysis and interpretation of data on phenomena that are not easily reduced or appropriately reduced to numbers or that may be misleading to research quantitatively.

How Qualitative Research applies to Health Care Research
Health care is just one area where these techniques are being applied, not only in the organization of health services, but also in the analysis of the interactions between doctors and patients and their relatives (Mays & Pope, 1995 (b)). This is also true of the study on the moment of death, where the interactions between doctor as researcher and the patient and relative evolves throughout the study, gradually developing trust between the patient, their families and the doctor, enriching both the quality of the study and the data obtained.

Qualitative research methods have a long history in science and medicine as well as in the social sciences and deserve to be recognized as an essential component in health and health services research. Although the more qualitative approaches found in the social sciences may seem alien alongside the experimental, quantitative methods used in clinical and biomedical research, as an essential component of health services research, they allow access to areas not amenable to the measurement figures of quantitative research. Indeed qualitative description can be regarded as a prerequisite of good quantitative research (Pope & Mays, 1995). Qualitative research can and does enrich our knowledge of health and health care in modern times.

Qualitative research has been described as situated activity that locates the observer in the world. It consists of a set of interpretive, material practices that makes the world visible. These practices turn the world into a series of representations including field notes, interviews, conversations, recordings and memos. At this level, qualitative research involves an interpretive, naturalistic approach to the world. Qualitative researchers study people in their natural settings, attempting to make sense of, or to interpret, phenomena in terms of the meaning people bring to them (Snape & Spencer, 2003). Qualitative research has been defined as the interpretive study of a specified issue or problem in which the researcher is central to the sense that participants make, a type of research that delivers findings not arrived at by statistical procedures or other means of quantification. (Banister, Burman & Parker, 1994; Strauss & Corbin, 1994). Qualitative research adopts assumptions about social life and involves documenting real events, recording what people say, observing specific behaviours, studying written documents or examining visual images. This type of research, focusing on subjective meanings, definitions, metaphors, symbols and description of specific cases aims to capture aspects of the social world for which it is difficult to develop precise measures expressed as numbers, as occurs in quantitative research (Neumann, 1997; Strauss and Corbin, (1994). It is the type of research that delivers findings not arrived at by statistical procedures or other means of quantification.

Narrative medicine and Qualitative Research
For many decades now, clinical physicians have been practicing narrative medicine, that is, medicine practiced with the narrative competence to recognize, interpret and be moved to action by the

predicament of others. Narratives and the telling of end of life stories by participants and relatives, is of vital relevance to palliative care physicians for over 50 years in helping to identify underlying issues for patients as well as those involved in their care. In a review of narratives written since 1950 by people facing death (Bingley, 2006), there is a clear awareness of social needs when dying, along with issues of communication with medical staff, symptom control, realities of suffering and spiritual aspects of dying. Researching stories told verbally and in writing is now well recognized as a valuable tool in the specialist methodological field within qualitative research (Bingley, Thomas & Brown, 2008; Donnelly (a) & (b) 1999). The growing acceptance of and demand for qualitative clinical research to complement quantitative clinical research, demonstrate for physicians the realization that both the singular and the statistically significant must be comprehended in the study of disease or its treatment (Charon R, 2001). These stories are a means through which participants define their lives, their identity, their culture and society. The stories of lives affected by illness may arise from a hope to enable a re-establishment of a continuity and sense of self, even in the face of death. (Bingley Thomas & Brown, 2008).

Qualitative Research in Palliative Medicine
Qualitative research is of more recent origin and becoming more widely known as a method of study and analysis in palliative medicine in contradistinction to that of the well established and universally accepted quantitative research. Its comparatively recent arrival as a method of research in Palliative Medicine is illustrated by the absence of any reference to qualitative research in either the first or second edition of the Oxford textbook of Palliative Medicine in 1993 and 1998 respectively. (Doyle, Hanks, 1993, 1998.). This study on the moment of death is an example of qualitative analysis in palliative medicine as applied to narratives. The study focuses on the narrative of families whose relatives have died a few weeks prior in a Specialist Palliative Care Unit.

Qualitative research places emphasis on the importance of the social context to understand the social world and in turn this context is a critical part of the qualitative research design. The meaning of a social action depends significantly on the context in which it appears. An event, social action, an answer to a question or conversation cannot be removed from the context in which it appears and the researcher ignores the social context at the risk of, distorting its social meaning and significance (Reetley, 2004). For this reason the setting of the moment of death study in a Palliative Care Unit is implicit to the stories told by the families.

In this study on the moment of death, detailed observation is taken by the researcher, of the patient and their family, weeks and months prior to death, and where interviews with family relatives takes place predominantly in the Palliative Care Unit at one week to six weeks after death. Questions asked of relatives at interview focus on the thoughts, feelings and actions of the patient and relatives at the moment of death.

In this present study on the moment of death, I use standard qualitative methods of obtaining data, through recording of interviews, listening to conversations, writing of field-notes and memos and I explain how and why people react and behave at this moment of death and so reveal what we do not know about this significant moment. The philosophy at the core of both qualitative and quantitative research should be that of "subtle realism"- an attempt to represent that reality. Qualitative research aims to be a representation rather than a reproduction of the truth being studied (Mays & Pope, 2000).

In this study I aim to take a snapshot view of relatives impressions of the needs and experiences of their dying relatives as well as their own needs and experiences. The study does not aim to be an exact replica of these truths but a representation. According to Denzin & Lincoln (1994), researchers who use qualitative research seek a deeper truth. They aim to study things in their natural setting, attempting to make sense of, or interpret phenomena in terms of the meanings people bring to them. They use a holistic perspective which preserves the complexities of human behaviour (Black 1994). Mays & Pope (1995), maintain that the goal of qualitative research is the development of concepts which help us to understand social phenomena in natural rather than experimental settings, giving due emphasis to the meanings, experiences and views of all the participants. The relatives' account of the experience of the moment of death is unique. Their observations and experiences capture the intimate reality of a single death, yet at the same time represents a universal truth. The meanings and interpretations which the bereaved relatives bring to the death of their relative, can be applied to all.

As Mays and Pope (2000) state, research is relevant when it adds to knowledge or increases the confidence with which existing knowledge is regarded. The moment of death study does both, by providing more knowledge than is previously known about the hour of death and by affirming the knowledge that already exists about the care provided for the dying and their relatives at the moment of death.

Qualitative versus Quantitative research
The most important test of any qualitative research is its quality. A good qualitative study can help us understand a situation that otherwise would be enigmatic or confusing. Evaluating quality in quantitative research does so, with a "purpose of explaining" while quality concept in qualitative research has a purpose of "generating understanding" (Golafshani, 2003). While, it is said that qualitative research tends to generate large amounts of detailed information about a small number of settings (Mays & Pope, 1995(a)), the most commonly held criticism of qualitative research is, that it comprises a mere assembly of anecdote and personal impressions, subject to researcher bias and that qualitative research lacks reproducibility. It is argued that the research being so personal to the researcher that there is no guarantee that a different researcher would come to radically different conclusions. The topic of researcher bias will be discussed in detail in Chapter 6 and how it applies to this study on the moment of death.

Mays and Pope, (1995 (a)), argue that in quantitative analysis it is possible to generate statistical representations of phenomena which may or may not be fully justified since, as in qualitative research they will depend on the judgement, skill and integrity of the researcher and the appropriateness to the question answered of the data collected. Mays and Pope (1995), define qualitative studies as those concerned with answering questions such as " What is X and how does X vary in different circumstances and why?" rather than "How many X's are there?" as in quantitative research. Qualitative research does not generally seek to enumerate. This is reiterated by Rose (1994), (under constant comp method, Hewitt Taylor, (2001) in describing the aim of qualitative research as portraying the reality of the area under investigation and enhancing understanding of the situation and the meanings and values attributed to this by individuals; it does not involve the quantification of facts. The above definitions concur with Bradley (1997) who states that the emphasis in qualitative research is on an accurate or true reflection of social reality (telling it like it really is) rather than on precision (saying how much it is like this or that).

Thus to this extent numbers are not of the essence in determining the worthiness or otherwise of a piece of research as Pope & Mays (1995), exemplify in their research on diabetes. In the treatment of this disease, there can be no doubt that quantitative methods, including randomized controlled trials have contributed to advances in the treatment of this disease. However, as well as proving that glycaemic control is effective in reducing long term complications of this disease, other questions need to be asked, particularly in relation to patient behaviour; knowing that the patient will comply with taking insulin is just as important as knowing that insulin is an effective treatment.

Peoples' experiences are subjective and cannot be adequately generalized or measured. Quantitative research fails to incorporate the value of therapeutic interactions, which are an integral part of caring, because it requires the researcher to be distanced from the participants (McLoughlin, 2002). The human experience cannot be adequately understood without the meanings and truths given to the experience by individuals (Guba & Lincoln, 1989). Qualitative research will never be wholly objective as it involves a close interactional relationship between participant and researcher.

The end-product of qualitative research is also more likely to be a better or clearer description of how things are, rather than predictive of how things might be. Qualitative research is more naturalistic and descriptive than experimental. Qualitative research methods can be used to generate descriptions and hypotheses and quantitative research methods can be used to test hypotheses. (Bradley, 1997).

In this study, I analyze by qualitative methods, patients and relatives' behaviour and the reasons they act in this way at the moment of death. I allow them to express their deepest concerns and needs at this time. Through my data analysis in this research, I aim to empower our responses and actions as professionals in accordance with the patient's and relative's needs at the moment of death. In Fig 2.1 Pope & Mays (1995), compare qualitative and quantitative methods of research:

Fig. 2.1

	Qualitative	**Quantitative**
Methods	Observation, Interview	Experiment, Survey
Question	What is X? (classification)	What is Y? (enumeration)
Reasoning	Inductive	Deductive
Strength	Validity	Reliability

Bradley (1997), demonstrates below corresponding terms describing trustworthiness of quantitative and qualitative research and all-embracing terms relating to the rigour underpinning all research.

Fig. 2.2

Quantitative	All-embracing term	Qualitative
Validity	Veracity	Credibility
Reliability	Consistency	Dependability
Objectivity	Neutrality	Conformability
Generalizability	Applicability	Transferability

According to Bradley (1997), both qualitative and quantitative methods attempt to be 'scientific', by which it is meant they seek to produce, an understanding of phenomena that is reasonably true and trustworthy. One has to look out for sources of bias and how these are dealt with and one seeks evidence of reliability and validity. In qualitative research, the corresponding concept to reliability that is repeatability-the same measurements should yield the same results time after time- is dependability, and corresponding to the strength of the concept of validity- the closeness to the truth- is the concept of credibility. The validity of qualitative methods is greatly enhanced by using a combination of research methods, a process known as triangulation and by independent analysis of the data by more than one researcher. These issues will be discussed later in this chapter. In failing to understand that quantitative and qualitative research yield different sorts of knowledge and to judge qualitative research by quantitative standards is a mistake (Bradley, 1997). The means of obtaining these concepts will be described later in detail. These methods include techniques such as triangulation, respondent validation and thick description the two latter methods not used in this moment of death study- (thick description includes giving complete tranches of unedited data, along with information on how they were condensed, edited or categorized so that the reader can arrive at their own judgement on the links between data and the model postulated (Bradley, 1997).

It is most important to understand that qualitative and quantitative research are not mutually exclusive but are rather complementary approaches which, when used together will usually reveal more about the world and how it works than will either used alone. The kind of knowledge produced by both endeavours is very different but neither type is in any absolute sense superior or inferior to the other and in the progress of medicine both types of knowledge are required (Bradley, 1997). Quantitative research begins with an idea, usually articulated as an hypothesis, which then through measurement, generates data and by deduction, allows a conclusion to be drawn. Qualitative research, in contrast, begins with an intention to explore a particular area, collects data by observations and interviews and generates ideas and hypotheses from these data, largely through what is known as inductive reasoning (Mays & Pope, 1996). quantitative research which seeks a single truth, qualitative studies through the involvement and interpretation of the voices of individuals, recognizes that there may be more than one "truth" in any given situation and seeks to describe them (Payne 1997). It is acknowledged in qualitative inquiry also that the researcher themselves because of their "immersion" in their chosen topic and the time spent with participants are unlikely to remain entirely detached from them. The researcher becomes part of the research process (Gantley 1999).

Clinical discourse and how its methods parallel with Qualitative Research

Miller and Crabtree (2005) propose a relationship between qualitative research methods and the clinical experience, the dialogue and the relationship between physician and patient. Even though qualitative research methods might still be viewed with suspicion and unease by many in clinical medicine, Miller and Crabtree show how qualitative research methods are the foundation of clinical discourse and the centuries- old relationship process between clinical physician and patient. The key is to recognize the similarity between the qualitative research process and the clinical process, particularly as it presents itself in primary care. This is demonstrated in Fig 2.3. The overall method consists of four separate processes: exploring, understanding, finding common ground and engaging in self-reflection. These four processes flow sequentially but they all iterate with each other and the whole process usually cycles multiple times over time, for any given illness episode.

Fig. 2.3

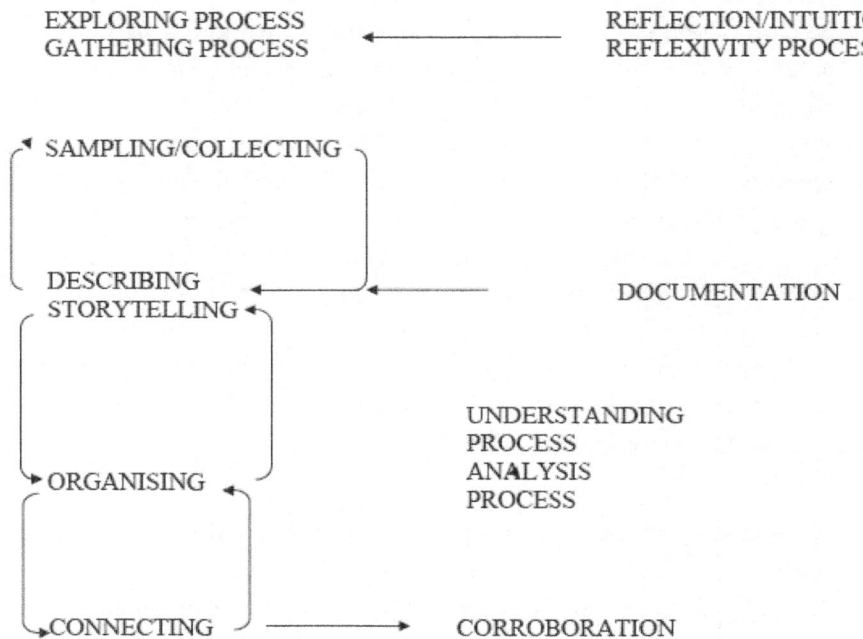

QUALITATIVE RESEARCH PROCESS AND CLINICAL PARALLEL

The four clinical processes directly correspond to the four processes of qualitative research. The clinician begins by gathering data, using purposeful or information-rich sampling. The clinician focuses his or her interviewing, observing and touching around possible explanations related to the patients presenting concern or opening story. The exploration seeks "disease" information, following the biomedical model, but like qualitative research, the process also searches for understanding of the patients health story and illness experience, especially the patients ideas, expectations and feelings about their concerns and the effect of their illness on their everyday lives. Like qualitative research the clinician almost immediately begins to analyze the data while continuing to gather additional information. This analysis seeks to understand the patients concern within the context of their own life-personal, family and community stories. In the clinical process using a participatory framework, the clinician periodically shares the emerging understanding with the patient and together they seek a common interpretation. Throughout this iterative process, the clinician is using self-reflection, personal feelings and intuition to inform the gathering, analyzing and interpreting of data. This is the basis of the qualitative researcher.

The visit ends when the clinician and patient agree that they have sufficient data - that is a saturation to implement an initial course of action. The outcome is an engaging plan for the patient and a report describing the encounter recorded (dictated) or written down (Miller & Crabtree, 2005). This is the process I engaged in as a qualitative researcher in this study on the moment of death.

Fig 2.4 demonstrates this qualitative study on the moment of death as applied to an idealized Relationship-Centred Clinical method. This understanding is organized around sensitizing concepts, diagnostic categories, personal experiences, connections, templates and scripts looked for and then corroborated against the known evidence. The above descriptions of clinical methods sound like, look like and feel like qualitative research. However most clinicians do not know it.

Qualitative Research in Health Science Research

Greenhalgh and Taylor (1997) describe several examples of the use of qualitative research. Questions such as "How many patients would consult their general practitioner when their child has a mild temperature?" or "What proportion of smokers have tried to give up?", clearly need answering through quantitative methods. But other questions such as "Why do parents worry so much about their children's temperature?" or "What stops people giving up smoking?" need to be answered through qualitative measures. We as qualitative researchers, need to listen to what people have to say and we should explore the ideas and concerns which the participants themselves come up with.

Fig. 2.4

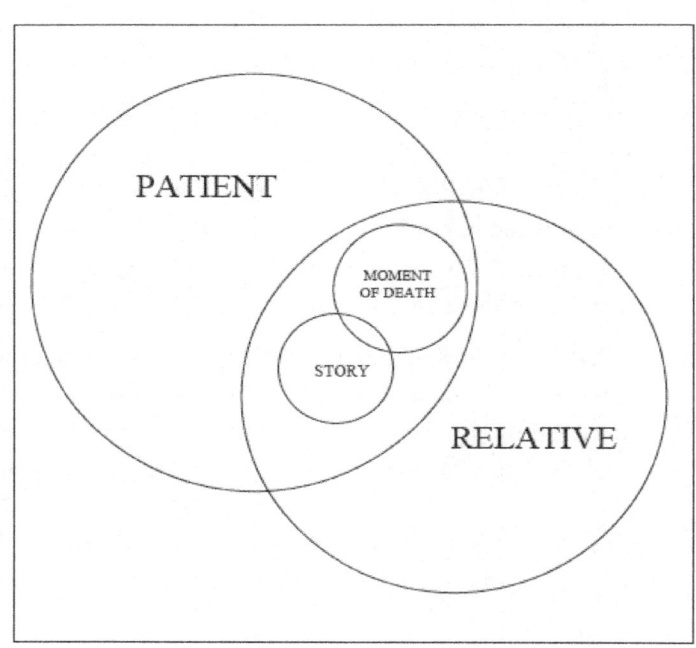

QUALITATIVE STUDY ON THE MOMENT OF DEATH AS APPLIED TO RELATIONSHIP-CENTRED CLINICAL METHOD.

QUALITATIVE RESEARCHER
SELF REFLECTION
INTUITION

By its very nature, qualitative research is non-standard, unconfined and dependant on the subjective experience of both the researcher and the researched (Greenhalgh & Taylor, 1997). . If the aim of the research is to determine the incidence of a disease or the frequency of an adverse drug reaction, or to show that a drug has a better risk-benefit ratio than another, a case control study, cohort study or randomised trial should be used. If however, the objective of the research is to explore, interpret, or obtain a deeper understanding of a particular clinical issue, qualitative methods are certainly the most appropriate ones to use (Greenhalgh & Taylor, 1997). Qualitative research is an iterative process. This means that there is an inherent flexibility in this approach which allows data collection and analysis to occur simultaneously. This in turn influences further sampling and data collection. (Kumar 1999).

Methods used in Qualitative Research: Sampling Methods

Deductive analysis is used mainly in quantitative research, analyzing data at specific stages of study. In quantitative research it is vital to ensure that a truly random sample of subjects is recruited so that the results reflect on average, the condition of the population from which the sample was drawn. In contrast by inductive reasoning or analysis, requires that the patterns, themes and categories of analysis are not pre-supposed and rather than being imposed on the data prior to data collection actually emerge from it. In this process the analyst moves back and forth between the logical construction and the actual data in a search for meaningful patterns (Dye, Schatz & Rosenburg (2000). The (inductive) iterative approach alters the research methods and the hypotheses as the study progresses, in the light of information found on the way and shows a commendable sensitivity to the richness and variability of the subject matter. (Greehalgh & Taylor, 1997). In qualitative research however, the researcher is not interested in an "on average" view of the population but wants to gain an in depth understanding of particular individuals or groups. As qualitative researchers we should therefore deliberately seek out individuals or groups who fit the bill (Greenhalgh & Taylor, 1997). Qualitative analysis as a consequence uses smaller sample sizes of individuals and the representativeness of even one participant is sufficient to provide valid results.

A commonly-used method of sampling in qualitative research is systematic, non-probabilistic, purposive, sampling. The purpose is not to establish a random or representative sample drawn from a population but rather to identify specific groups of people who either possess characteristics or live in circumstances relevant to the social phenomenon being studied. Informants are identified because they will enable exploration of a particular aspect of behaviour relevant to the research. A wide range of informants are used in order to select key informants with access to important sources of knowledge (Mays & Pope, 1995 (a). The idea of this type of sampling is not to generalize to the whole population but to indicate common links or categories shared between the setting observed and others like it. At its most powerful, the single case can demonstrate features or provide categories relevant to a wide number of cases and applies to the selection process of this moment of death study. Even though the sample selected was small each family in the study represents a single unique story and each patient reveals in turn more information about the moment of death in the Palliative Care Unit. Each patient and family demonstrating features and providing categories relevant to the general population. I chose purposive sampling in this study. I used a method by which a deliberate choice of respondents were made. In the Palliative Care Unit, patients were selected by myself as researcher and a member of the Pastoral Care team. The Pastoral Care team member had had initial contact with the patient and their relatives on admission, then informed me of patients and relatives or carers that suited the following criteria:

1. The doctors considered patients had less than 6 months to live.
2. The patient had at least one visiting carer or relative.
3. The patient was likely to die in the Palliative Care Unit (as shown by expressed preference or desire.)

Relatives and carers were selected by me when identified as visiting the patient on a regular basis. I was able to establish a relationship with the family member or carer over several weeks and months. I learned more of the personality of the patient and what their daily life and family life was like. I could not always converse with the patient if they were too ill, but I could get to know them through the eyes of the relative or carer. This relationship with the relative or carer was nurtured throughout the study until at the time of the interview it was not an unusual, stressful formality but simply another easy conversation with the relative. Even though the sampling selection might appear biased due to the confined setting in a Specialist Palliative Care Unit, this setting was chosen as it is one of the most natural settings for death to occur in modern Ireland. Any possible bias in selecting participants in this study is discussed further in Chapter 6.

Observation in Qualitative Research
The qualitative researcher systematically listens to and watches people and events to learn about behaviours and interactions in their natural settings. This involves the systematic, detailed observation of behaviour and talk, watching what people do and recording what they say. The crucial point is that this observation takes place its natural setting as opposed to an experimental one. This is exemplified, in my moment of death study, in the Palliative Care Unit. In an attempt to minimize the effect of intrusion into the environment of grief and mourning, I become a "participant-observer" involved in the activities taking place while observing them. There is mutual awareness of the research, by researcher and participant. (Mays & Pope, 1995 (b)). I concur with Bradley (1997), when he states that observation in qualitative research is never either entirely participant, or entirely non-participant, in that in order to gain people's trust sufficiently to understand them one must to some degree give up one's objective stance. Participation or non-participation is never absolute, but is always just a matter of degree. By sitting with both dying patients and their family relatives on a daily basis for many hours over many months in the Palliative Care Unit, I, as researcher took the role of participant and observer, I became fully aware of the patient's and family's needs and concerns leading up to and surrounding the moment of death. On a daily basis, I was able to document in field notes, that which I had seen and heard and to which I had appended an account of my impressions and thoughts, allowing to collect and analyse data simultaneously throughout, from the first day of research. It is important to be aware however of the effect that the "participant as observer" role can have on the participant, known as

the "Hawthorne effect". According to Mays & Pope (1995 (a)& (b)), having a researcher observing actions may stimulate modifications or changes in behaviour or action.

I did not notice the Hawthorne effect in this study. Albeit without the customary white coat, I did notice initially on introducing myself to a patient and their family, as a medical doctor doing research, that |I was met with a cool and reserved reaction on the mention of the word "research". On consultation with my supervisor, I decided henceforth to exclude the term "research" and introduce myself as a medical doctor who was aiming to improve the overall care of patients and their families. This introduction produced a much warmer and open response from the patients and their families. Having overcome the barrier of introduction, with the exception of one family, I found all families, welcomed and trusted me as a researcher. One family, in particular were aggressive and angry, primarily, I felt, due to their father's illness. |I do not believe this reaction was the effect of my research, as their anger, mainly due to grief extended to many of the staff attending to their father.

Bias in Qualitative Research
In order to conduct valid research, it is imperative that the researcher be aware of his or her own cultural perspective, bias or agenda (Morse & Field, 1995). According to Greenhalgh & Taylor (1997), it is important to recognize that there is no way of abolishing, or fully controlling, observer bias in qualitative research. In qualitative studies, researchers view bias as unavoidable and they are likely to state their biases openly (Maione, 1997). Brody (1992), argues that since the naturalistic investigator is the researcher as a research instrument, naturalistic inquiry cannot avoid observer bias by using the instrument to insulate the experiment from the preconceptions of the investigator. Instead, open disclosure of preconceptions and assumptions that may have influenced data gathering and processing becomes an inherent part of the conduct of the inquiry. This is most obviously the case when participant observation is used, as in this study on the moment of death, but it is also true for other forms of

data collection and quantitative analysis. Greenhalgh & Taylor (1997) give the following example:

In research undertaken on the experience of asthmatic adults living in damp and overcrowded housing and the perceived effect of these surroundings on their health, the data generated through focus groups or semi-structured interviews are likely to be heavily influenced by what the interviewer believes on the subject or whether the researcher is employed by the hospital chest clinic or an environmental pressure group. In these situations the researcher should describe in detail their beliefs about what might influence data collection, so the results can be interpreted accordingly.

In this study on the moment of death, sampling bias, interview bias and researcher bias are three key areas where bias must be strictly controlled. I will discuss these issues in greater depth in Chapter 8.

Validity in Qualitative Research
One important method of reducing if not eliminating bias from a qualitative study is ensuring validity. Validity can be defined as the extent to which a measurement truly reflects the phenomenon under scrutiny and whether this truth accurately reflects the real situation (Pope & Mays, 1995 (c); Guion, 2002). It is necessary therefore, when assessing the validity of a qualitative research study, to ask whether the interpretation placed on the data accords with common sense and is relatively untainted with cultural or personal perspective (Greenhalgh & Taylor, 1997). This can be a difficult exercise, because the language we use to describe things tends to imply meanings and motives which the subjects themselves may not share. There are several methods available in order to achieve this:

(i) Triangulation
Triangulation involves using methods to ensure validity in qualitative research. It compares the results from either two or more different methods of data collection, for example, interviews, observation and document analysis. If the findings from all of the methods draw the

same or similar conclusions, then validity in the finding has been established (Guion, 2002). The researcher looks for patterns of convergence to develop or corroborate an overall interpretation (Pope & Mays, 1995). Part of this method to ensure validity, includes techniques in which the investigators account is compared with that of other researchers or a supervisor. If the findings from the different evaluators arrive at the same conclusion, then validity has been established (Guion, 2002). This method of triangulation using several methods of data collection, that is interviews, observation and field-notes and diaries were used in this moment of death study and a supervisor and external consultant researcher's interpretation of the study were also used, thus ensuring validity.

(ii) Reflexivity
Reflexivity is another method by which validity of the study is ensured. It is a process in which sensitivity is maintained to the methods by which the researcher and the research process have shaped and collected the data, including the role of prior assumptions and experiences. Personal and intellectual biases need to be made plain at the outset of any research reports to enhance the credibility of the findings (Mays & Pope, 2000). Mays & Pope, (1996) suggest three useful questions for determining validity.

How well does the analysis explain why people behave in the way they do?
In this study, throughout the interviews, the relatives of the dying tell and explain their own stories. Their accounts are self-explanatory and reveal slowly why they behave in the way they do. Direct quotes used in the findings of the study, illuminate individual family members thoughts and actions, the reasons behind those actions and provide the foundation and support for my final conclusions in the study.

How comprehensible would the explanation of the conclusions of the study be to a thoughtful participant in the setting?

The quotes in the findings of this study on the moment of death are taken directly from the family interviews. They are in the families own words. They share a common experience of the moment of death and so the findings would be most comprehensible to them.

How well does the explanation cohere with what we already know?

There are many universal themes on the topic of death and dying, extracted from the interview quotes. They are universal themes of significance in the process of death and dying for the present but have relevance in many cultures and traditions from the past and will have for the future.

According to Mays & Pope (1995 (a)) the report of a qualitative study should carry sufficient conviction to enable someone else to have the same experience as the original observer and appreciate the truth of the account. For this reason and also to ensure validity, in the moment of death study, my supervisor, read and re-read all transcripts, read all diaries and independently analysed the data as it was collected. I also met with my external researcher, David Clark, who is Professor of Medical Sociology at Lancaster University, UK, and visiting Professor of Hospice Studies at Trinity College, Dublin and University College, Dublin, on several occasions, to discuss and independently analyse the data and interviews.

Validation by Respondents

Another method of ensuring validity is the interpretation of the responses and emergent findings with participants (Hewitt-Taylor, 2001). This method is praised by Nolan & Behi (1995), who suggest that in qualitative research, findings should be presented to participants and their views explored. However, Silverman (1993) claims that this procedure does not fully validate the findings and might only mean that the interpretation given is acceptable to respondents. Riley (1990) affirms this by stating that although achieving a balance of power is important, respondents should not be given too much power in relation to defining the research interpretations. I chose not to use respondent validation in the moment of death study. I considered it sufficient validation to confirm and analyse the meaning and interpretation of what was said during the interview itself. I did this by questioning and repeating any ambivalent answers given by respondent in order to clarify meaning. I felt it inappropriate and unnecessary for the grieving relatives to return at a later date for further validation.

Attention to negative cases
A long established test for improving validity in qualitative research is to search for and discuss elements in the data that contradict, or seem to contradict the emerging explanation of the phenomena under study. Such "deviant case analysis" helps refine the analysis (Mays & Pope, 2000). The key to developing rigorous and valid theory using the constant comparative method lies in this search for "deviant "cases which contained within the researchers data, are searched as exceptions to the emerging relations between codes. A full report of qualitative analysis should account for "deviant" cases and how they have contributed to refining theory (Green, 1998).

As all interviews of families revealed data reflecting the needs, specific to each patient and their families the concept of showing "deviant cases" was not applicable to my moment of death study. It was difficult for a story to be "deviant" or contrary to the overall results as every family member presented their stories specific to their situation. Each family acted as their own controls in expressing their unique comments, observations, ideas and concerns.

Interviewing in Qualitative research
Kvale (1996) presents the qualitative research interview as characterized by a methodological awareness of question forms, a focus on the dynamics of interaction between interviewer and interviewee and a critical attention to what is said. The author

continues to state that qualitative research interviews are used to develop knowledge that may change persons or conditions. The personal interaction in the interview affect the interviewee and the knowledge produced by an interview affects our understanding of the human situation.

Both qualitative and quantitative researchers tend to rely on the interview as the basic method of data gathering for the purpose of obtaining a rich in depth experiential account of an event or episode in the life of the respondent. There is inherent faith that the results are trustworthy and accurate and that the relation of the interviewer to the respondent that evolves during the interview process has not unduly biased the account (Atkinson, 1997; Silverman, 1993).

Structured interviewing

In structured interviewing as used in this study on the moment of death, the interviewer asks each of the respondents the same series of pre-established questions. The only room for variation in response from the respondent is when open-ended questions are used. All respondents receive the same set of questions asked in the same order or sequence. The following principles apply for the interviewer in the structured interview:

Never get involved in long explanations of the study. Use the standard explanation as provided by the supervisor. Never deviate from the study introduction, sequence of questions or question wording.

Never suggest an answer or agree or disagree with an answer. Do not give personal views on the topic or the questions. *(Fontana & Frey, 2005).*

The first source of error in structured interviews is respondent behaviour. The respondent may deliberately try to please the interviewer or prevent the interviewer from learning something about them which they do not wish to reveal. The respondent may also err due to faulty memory (which is likely to occur and is unavoidable in this moment of death study due to the grief of the participants.) Another source of error can be on the part of the interviewer whose characteristics or questioning techniques might impede proper communication (Bradburn, 1983).

However, according to Fontana & Frey (2005) the overall impact of the interviewer on response quality in structured interviews is minor, directly attributable to the inflexible, standardized and predetermined nature of this type of interviewing. The authors Fontana & Frey (2005) state that there is simply little room for error.

Empathetic Interviewing

Empathetic interviewing emphasizes taking a stance contrary to the scientific image of interviewing which is based on the concept of neutrality. Indeed much of traditional interviewing concentrates on the language of scientific neutrality and the techniques to achieve it. (Fontana & Frey, 2005)

As many have argued convincingly (Atkinson & Silverman, 1997; Fontana, 2002; Holstein & Gubrum,1995; Scheurich ,1995), interviewing is not merely the neutral exchange of asking questions and getting answers. Two or more people are involved in this process and their exchanges lead to the collaborative effort called the interview. The key here is the "active" nature of this process, that leads to a contextually bound and mutually created story- the interview.

In a research setting, it is the responsibility of the interviewer to get beyond merely a polite conversation or exchange of ideas. The interviews must establish an atmosphere in which the subject feels safe to talk about their feelings. In my moment of death study, relatives were assured of this safeness to talk, by the privacy of an interview room in the Palliative Care Unit, where there were no disturbances or in the privacy of their own home. Allowing the interviewee express their feelings freely, involves a delicate balance between cognitive knowledge seeking and the ethical aspects of emotional human interaction (Spradely,1979).

As Spradely (1979) advocates, I, as the research interviewer, use myself as a research instrument, allowing a privileged access to the subjects living world. The interview becomes the raw material and the decisive factor for the quality of later analysis and it is essential that the meaning of what is said is interpreted, verified and communicated by the time the tape-recorder is switched off.

The quality criteria in the interview setting include:
> The extent to which there are spontaneous, rich, specific and relevant answers from the interviewee.

The degree to which there are short interviewer questions and long interviewee answers, The degree to which the interviewer follows up and clarifies the meanings of answers during the interview.

That the interview is self-communicating- it is a story contained in itself and does not require much more description and explanations *(Spradely, 1979)*.

The above criteria were applied by me to the moment of death interviews. As Hynson & Aroni (2006) state in their qualitative in-depth interviews of bereaved parents, careful attention to the research process in terms of timing, approach and the interviewer's skills were key elements that underpinned an overall positive experience. Increasingly qualitative researchers are realizing that interviews are not neutral tools of data gathering but rather active human interactions between people leading to negotiated, contextually based results. Thus the focus of interviews is moving to encompass the how's of people lives as well as the traditional what's (the activities of everyday life) (Dingwall R. 1997; Kvale 1996; Seidman, 1991; Silverman 1993; Silverman 1997a).

Fontana & Frey (2005), state that the latest trends in interviewing have come some distance from structured questions. There is a realization for some time that researchers are not invisible neutral entities. Researchers are realizing that they cannot lift the results of their interviews out of the contexts in which they were gathered and claim them as objective data with no strings attached. They are part of the interaction they seek to study and it cannot be denied that they influence that interaction merely by their presence. (Fontana & Frey, 2005). In this study, I as researcher and interviewer used a combination of empathetic and structured interviewing. I showed natural empathy with the bereaved yet allowed for detachment by not deviating from formal structured questioning and by not becoming overly-personal in any way in my interactions. According to Fontana & Frey (2005), qualitative research interviews are like snapshots, providing a picture taken during a moment in time. The interviews gain a view of research participants concerns as they present them, rather than as events unfold. The authors also state that it must be acknowledged that each interview is unique and cannot be replicated in either another interview or in a repeat interview with the same participant. It is the uniqueness of each interview which tells each participants story, painting his or her picture and will be of interest to others (Fontana & Frey, 1998). McLoughlin (2002) informs us that interviews of this nature enables the researcher to gain richer insights into the participants 'life world'.

Another term for the interviews used in this moment of death study are focused interviews. Focused interviews, are conversations in which the interviewee talks and the interviewer listens, responds and encourages. In this study on the moment of death, bereaved relatives were allowed to speak with minimal interruption by me as interviewer. In this way, relatives are allowed to listen to their own ideas evolving and in doing so providing richness and depth to the interview. Jean-Francois Lyotard (1984) explains aptly in his writings "...... that for us a language is first and foremost someone talking. But there are language games in which the important thing is to listen....and in this game, one speaks only in as much as one listens, that is, one speaks as a listener....."

The interviewer must listen to the content of what is being said and also must be aware of the process of the interview. The interviewer must encourage the participants to interrupt the interview with anything they think is important. The interviewer must listen actively focusing on verbal and nonverbal cues. Probing by the interviewer can include questions used for elaboration "Can you tell me more about that?" or "What happened then?" or for clarification "I am not sure I understand what you mean by that."(HSR, 2002). The use of interviews in a study allow for flexibility, clarification of language and meaning and they permit further probing where appropriate (Parchoo, 1997; Avis, 1997).

I chose the face-to-face interview as a method in order to be fully present with relatives as they told their stories, to experience their emotions, reactions and feelings at first hand and to gain as much insight as possible into their firsthand experience of their relatives' moment of death.

From my experience interviewing bereaved families in the moment of death study and conversing at length with dying patients, I concur fully with Kellehear (1989) who states that interviewing patients with life-threatening illness by a researcher with a clinical background is not only valuable and ethical but in addition produces a positive therapeutic benefit. There is evidence that patients derive benefit from the experience of talking to a researcher and appreciate the opportunity to be listened to or to help others (Hudson, 2003; Payne, 1997; Plant, 1996)

I was conscious of not having a clinical responsibility to the interviewees and although I was aware of not allowing the interview to become a therapeutic situation many interviewees expressed to me how they had felt better after the interview. In response to the interview setting, I found relatives very forthcoming in talking about their grief and their loss and particularly about the moment of death of their relative. No family was resistant to talking about these subjects. Some however showed anger in their grief, but this was to be expected and was not directed solely at me as researcher but to other members of staff. (Initially I found it difficult as an interviewer not to personalise the anger shown but on discussion with my supervisor I learnt to understand the anger shown in grief). I found younger members of families talked less about their grief and the moment of death of their relative than older members. As a researcher I had to be on my guard against any personal bias on my part, during the interviews. The issue of Bias and the Interview process in this study will be discussed further in detail under Method in Chapter 6.

Once we, as researchers, accept our natural human interactions with respondents, recognize our bias and take measures to safeguard against them, we can produce fruitful, enriching and valid results while still reflecting our humanity.

Field-notes and researcher diary

Crabtree & Miller (1992) have stated that before entering the field, it is important for the researcher to record their feelings, hunches, known biases, assumptions and even expected outcomes. According to the authors, doing so provides a baseline against which the researcher can compare with what actually emerges as the study develops. As researcher, I chose to maintain a field diary or record of the research process to detail events, personal reactions to events and changes to my views over time. In this moment of death study I chose to use two diaries. One to record personal interpretations, the other to record the progression of the study itself or any changes to the course of the collection of data or the analysis. This method concurs with also, who claim that this forms a basis for tentative hypotheses or the evolution of systems of classification (Mays & Pope, 1995 (b)). This method also allows the researcher to become aware of and analyse his or her bias as I did in this study on the moment of death.) In this study I recorded field-notes of an interview in the home of Mrs P whose husband had died in the SPCU two weeks earlier. (see Chapter 7 on Fieldnotes for other examples.)

"I travelled to Mrs P's home. The housing estate had a dishevelled appearance and most of the houses looked poor. I found Mrs P's house eventually. It was an unassuming house at the end of a row of houses in a cul de sac. On answering the door Mrs P looked worn and tired. She invited me into her home into the living room. A young pretty fair-haired girl, Mrs P's daughter, offered me a cup of tea. I accepted gratefully. I sympathized with them both on the loss of their husband and father respectively. I had heard and had experienced myself on meeting the family once before in the SPCU that they were "difficult to deal with".

For this reason I was on my guard. I explained once again to the family as I had explained previously in the SPCU of the purpose of my visit to their home, the interview and the use of the tape recorder. Mrs P signed the consent form. As I switched on the tape recorder, Mrs P spoke of the loss of her husband. As she spoke her daughter returned with tea and biscuits. Her daughter D began to speak with a certain forcefulness and anger with intermittent laughter about members of staff who had attended her father in the SPCU.

D dismissed members of staff as inept and of no help to her father or the family. I sat there and said little. I found it difficult as I knew each member of the staff well and knew how hard they had worked and had cared for Mr P……Mrs P and her daughter continued to speak of the days and weeks before Mr P's death.

They said that at Mr P's death his family "whipped him off" that "they came for him" and they felt that he was talking to his dead sister before he died. The daughter said that in her dreams she saw his dead sister come up in a black car, but she never opened the garden door, so she didn't come in. Then she said the knocking started at the door at home every morning at six o' clock. Mrs P stated that her husband did" the rounds" when he was in the coma, that he went to all the places that he loved……"

On recording field-notes by hand during this study, I concluded that it was important to do so immediately where my observations were fresh in my mind. I also needed to do this in the quiet of my office with no interruptions and to write freely as I remembered my observations.

Use of Computers in Qualitative Research
Computer packages such as NUD*ist and ATLAS.ti are of use in the analysis of data in qualitative research. These packages help to sort data, when coding and gathering themes. I used in my study on the moment of death, a slower but still as effective method in sorting data,

using coloured wall charts, where themes were grouped and sorted manually on these large charts and cut and pasted either on the charts or on Windows XL.

Transferability
Transferability involves demonstrating the applicability of the results of the study in one context to other contexts. This can be enhanced by providing what is called thick description, that is, giving enough detail, so the readers can decide for themselves if the results are transferable to their own contexts. Marshall & Rossman (1989) note that transferability is the responsibility of the person seeking to apply the results of the study to a new context, that is, it is the responsibility of the reader. It is the responsibility of the researcher to provide sufficient descriptive detail. In this enquiry into the moment of death, I provide sufficient detail in the results, demonstrating universal themes about death and dying that apply to the deathbed scene throughout the world. Amongst many issues raised are human needs for dignity, presence, touch, accompaniment, prayer, vigil, lay and professional care and freedom from pain. The transferability of this study are in the words spoken by the dying and their relatives. Their words resonate with us all.

Data Analysis in Qualitative Research
Reliability in data analysis is the extent to which a measurement yields the same answer each time it is used (Pope & Mays, 1995 (c)) This term can also be called "exhaustiveness", where similar themes are emerging over and over again by participants. This is also a description of a constant comparative method of analysis that is used in qualitative research (Steinhauser & Clipp, 2000). I chose the constant comparative method of analysis in the moment of death study as I believe its methods are the most suitable to my methods used for collecting data, by observation, field-notes and interview transcripts and a method most suitable to obtaining the maximum interpretation of the rich data collected. As Hewitt-Taylor (2001)

reminds us, the constant comparative method can be used with a single method of data collection or where multiple data collection methods are used as in the moment of death study.

Once the interviews have been read and re-read, and then transcribed, the significance of their analysis are revealed by the agreement and repetition of themes isolated by specific family groups or by contrasting observations by individuals which irrespective of whether they are complex, simple or epiphanic, serve to assert their independence from the rest (Hewitt-Taylor, 2001).

The constant comparative method is the method I chose to isolate and compare these themes. I, as researcher was fully aware of possible bias in isolating themes from interviews that seemed more interesting or by favouring one interview over another. Once aware of this tendency to bias, all interviews and data analysed, were treated equally, with the same thoroughness and rigour and read and re-read by myself and my supervisor and an external researcher.

The constant comparative method analyses qualitative data where the information gathered is coded into emergent themes or codes. All information gathered during the study are read and re-read. All transcripts are given a code number and identifying information removed in order to maintain anonymity (Williams & Payne, 2003). In this study on the moment of death, data collected included interview transcripts, observational notes, researcher diaries and field diaries. The data is constantly assessed after initial coding until it is clear that no new themes are emerging (Hewitt-Taylor, 2001). Each coding category is read and conceptually organized to identify the major emergent themes. Concepts are those that describe discrete happenings, events and phenomena. Categories are a classification of concepts, the concepts grouped together under a named category. It is important to note that analysis seeks to promote understanding of individual perceptions and not to prove a preconceived theory. Codes are therefore generated from the data and not predetermined (Hewitt-Taylor, 2001). The founders of the constant comparative method, Glaser & Strauss, (Glaser & Strauss,1967) state that the method facilitates the generation of complex 'theories of process, sequence and change pertaining to organizations, positions and social interactions that correspond closely to the data since the constant comparison forces the analyst to consider much diversity in the data'. The researcher should become thoroughly familiar with the data, be sensitive to the context of the data, be prepared to extend, change and discard categories, consider connections and avoid needless overlaps and record the criteria on which category decisions are to be taken.

The quality of data analysis depends on repeated, systematic searching of the data (Hammersley, 1981). In an attempt to achieve this, as in the moment of death study, repeated coding was performed to review interpretations, in light of the new data gathered and as the new codes were generated, until no new insights were being gleaned (Williams & Payne, 2003). Established coded sections were compared with other similarly coded segments to ensure consistency of application, as well as adherence to the definition of the code (Strauss & Corbin, 1990). During the course of the analysis, the criteria for including and excluding observations, are vague at the beginning becoming more precise (Dey, 1993). As previously mentioned data collection and analysis are interwoven in qualitative research (Hewitt-Taylor, 2001). Successful analysis and presentation of qualitative data requires a systematic and ordered approach so that complex data that emerge from a variety of sources can be collated and presented in manageable form. Interviews are continued until theoretical saturation is achieved where no new themes are identified and nothing new added to what has already been elicited during ongoing analysis (Williams & Payne, 2003). In this study theoretical saturation was achieved after 20 interviews.

In this study on the moment of death, one of the main emerging categories was the moment of death itself (after reading and re-reading the twenty interview transcripts by my supervisor and I). From this category a range of further sub-categories were isolated, common sub-categories united and broken down further into themes. A subcategory can be defined as the answer to questions about the phenomenon or category previously isolated. These questions include how, when, where, why and with what consequences. Dignity emerged as a subcategory of the phenomenon of the moment of death in an answer to the question - how did this moment of death occur. Dignity as a subcategory was divided into further themes such as such as the desire of the patient and family for dignity and how that dignity was given by all staff, including catering staff, doctors, nurses and Pastoral Care. Also the simple acts that demonstrated dignity, such as the act of being washed and dressed, combing of the hair, presence of the family, talking with the dying person, holding their hand and embracing them.

Another example of a category common to all the interviews is that of vigil. From this, subcategories formed, answered the questions how, when, why and with what consequences. These subcategories included, ritual, presence, accompaniment and community. Further themes isolated from these are the waiting by the dying person for a family member, touch, prayer and detailed descriptions of last breaths of the dying person. I will discuss the analysis of this study on the moment of death further under study analysis in Chapter 6.

Fig 2.5 The Constant Comparative Method

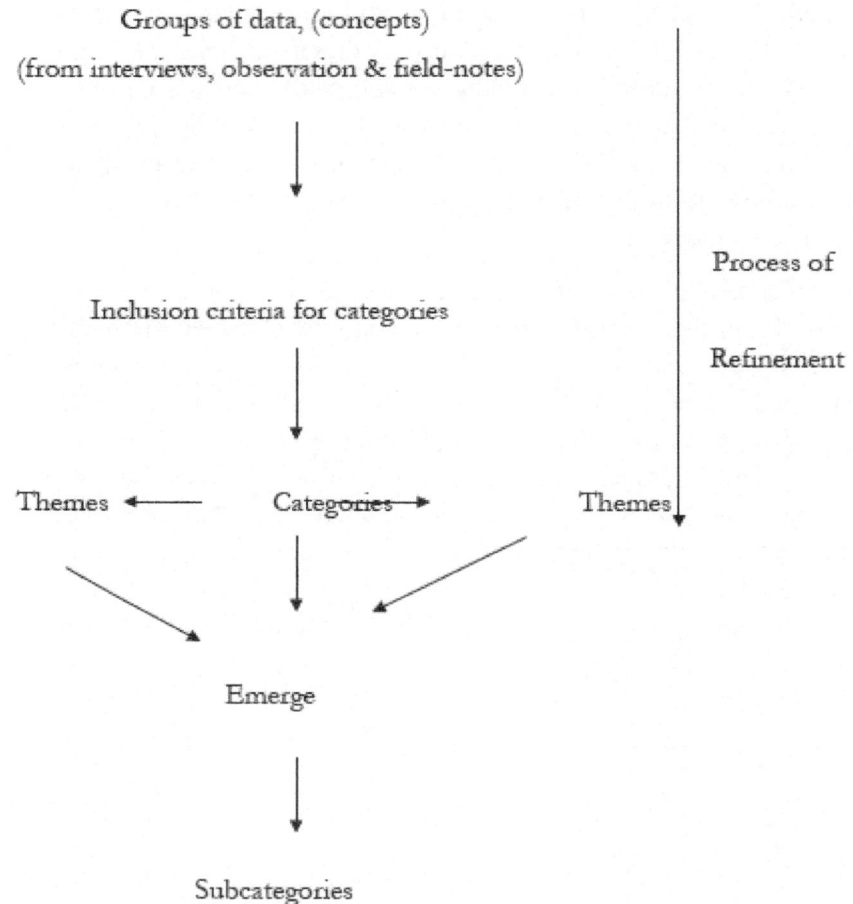

(Dye, Schatz & Rosenberg, 2000)

The basis on which the interview quotes are chosen are as follows:

Large categories are demonstrated by extracting quotes directly from the interviews. Themes emerge from these categories and are grouped. Subcategories are thus formed asking the questions who, what, were, when, how and with what consequences events occurred.

All categories and themes are represented by direct quotes as in the findings of this study See Fig 2.6 (a) & (b).

Five stages of data analysis used in this study on the Moment of Death

Reading of data, transcripts of interviews, observation notes and field-log diaries consistently throughout the study. Collection of data and analysis occurs concurrently from beginning of study. Identifying all key issues and concepts. Constant referral to the aims and objectives of the study is important at this stage. Indexing and coding data. Labelling quotes from transcripts and coding to extract themes.

Creating charts for each interview. Charting rearranges the data according to the appropriate part of the thematic framework to which they relate (Pope & Mays, 2000). There is a chart for each key subject area or theme with entries for several respondents. Unlike simple cut and paste methods that group verbatim text, the charts contain distilled summaries of views and experiences (Pope & Mays, 2000). On wallpaper charts I drew out graphs and diagrams of categories and subcategories from one interview, isolating themes. Each chart created represented an interview with one family. Each chart with its categories and themes was cross-referenced with the next interview chart and so on. This stage of analysis can also be done by using computer packages NUD*ist or ATLAS.ti. In this study I chose to group themes and form new subcategories by hand, using the charts.

All themes are finally arranged in their subcategories and the search for new themes from all interviews is exhausted.

It is not normally appropriate to write up qualitative research in the conventional format of a scientific paper, with a rigid distinction between the results and the scientific account as these are interwoven due to simultaneous data collection and analysis. Quantitative research, however, usually presents each section distinctively, presented in the methods section, numerical tables and the accompanying commentary.

Qualitative research depends in much larger part on producing a convincing account and is more descriptive in its narrative form (Mays & Pope, (a)). In this qualitative enquiry, from the interviews with relatives, one week after death of the patient, descriptive narratives and direct quotes are used in the analysis section. The results in this moment of death study through the use of direct quotes from the relatives of those who died provides a window into the lives of these people and allows us experience with them the hours at and surrounding the moment of death.

The Use of the Constant Comparative method in Data Analysis:

Example of analysis in this study on the Moment of Death

Fig 2.6 (a) Groups of Data (concepts)

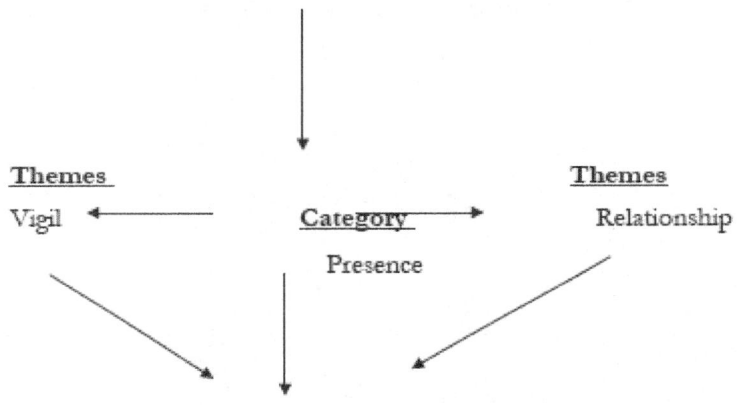

Subcategories/ Subthemes relating to Presence

Prayer & Ritual: "I said to my wife you start the rosary. She started the rosary. The lovely prayers took a lot of the grief away Accompaniment: " He knew we were there." Community: "Her brother, husband, sister-in-law, nephew and niece were there."

The dying person waiting for family: "She waited for PJ to come home...... she was doing it for him."

Fig 2.6 (b) Groups of Data

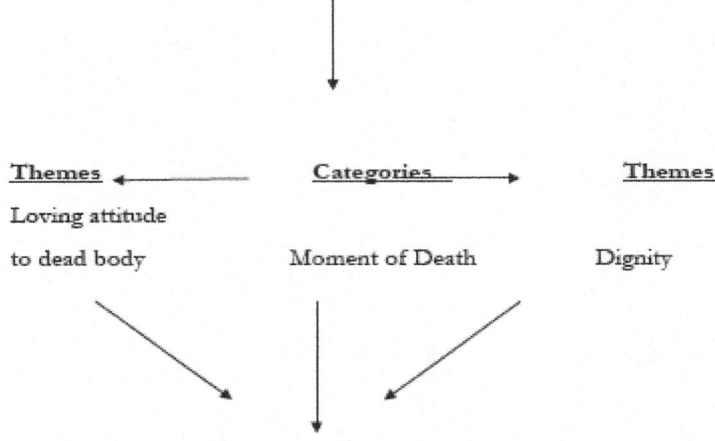

Prayer and Ritual: "There were some lovely prayers and that took a lot of the grief away"

Accompaniment: "We all roared at him "We love you" and we know that was the last thing he heard"

Humour: "John said, sure we may as well let down the mattress as the mattress was still pumped up and I thought God she's still alive...... and we were giggling. I didn't realise it, it was the bed.

Chapter 3:
The Concept of a "Good Death":
An Exploration

As the medical community focuses on the need to improve the quality of care at the end of life, it becomes increasingly important to identify those areas of care that are most important to dying patients and their families. Addressing patient and family perceptions of their needs may help to reverse the slow progress to date in implementing interventions effective in improving end of life care especially in teaching and general hospitals (Wenrich & Curtis, 2003). This qualitative study on the moment of death in a Specialist Palliative Care Unit seeks to address these needs.

Good care for dying patients has always been an obligation in medicine. To fulfill this obligation, physicians must embrace the integralness of dying in life, must recognise when to submit to dying with equanimity and must develop attentive and individualized plans of care for each patient (Berger, Rosner & Potash, 2000). The palliative care movement has challenged the prevailing death-denying attitude of the present health-care system and championed a positive attitude to caring for dying patients and their relatives at this vulnerable time. To bestow the accumulated knowledge of this model of care a greater focus is needed on the educational issues involved in the diagnosis and treatment of dying as a complex human process. As Ellershaw & Ward (2003) state, expertise in the care of the dying patient needs to be disseminated widely.

Palliative medicine must continue to develop compassionate, individually tailored and effective responses to the mounting vulnerability and increasingly difficult physical, psychosocial and spiritual challenges facing persons nearing the end of life (Chochinov, 2006) and the effect this dying has on close relatives. In our world of increasingly sophisticated medical technology, there is growing concern that the humanity of the care of persons facing death is lost and consequently the care needed is wanting (Feinberg, 1997).

Traditions of death and dying in Ireland

In the past, people were as familiar with death as they were with life and death was a natural extension of life. In view of people's oneness with nature and the spiritual world, death was not to be feared. The acceptance of death as the one truism of life, was facilitated by a strong faith in the after-life and prayer in people for whom in the celebration of death, humour was never far away (Donnelly, 1999 (a).

In Ireland the culture of death changed dramatically in initially the urban and then the rural areas during the 20th century. When people died primarily at the single-handed family doctor, home, family, clergy and particularly the community assumed responsibility. As the location of death shifted to the hospital, physicians became the gate keepers. As a result, death is now viewed through the lens of biomedical explanation and is primarily described as a physiological event (Steinhauser, 2000). In the eighteenth century dying was constructed as such a key transition that a craft of dying was developed in Christian literature which included a complete and intelligible guide to the business of dying, a method to be learned while one was in good health (O 'Connor, 1966). In the Ars Moriendi tradition a ritual drama was enacted at the site of the deathbed in which the living kept vigil and administered the last rites and the person who was dying engaged in battle between the forces of good and evil (Bell, 2005; O' Connor, 1966) This ritual is reflected in this study on the moment of death by the use of ritual, with crucifix, blessed candle and holy water in all the death bed scenes.

A strictly biomedical perspective is incomplete. For those involved with the care of the dying, death has a broader meaning and is considered a natural part of life, not a failure of technology. Steinhauser (2000) also states that for the dying person and their families, psychosocial and spiritual issues are as important as physiological concerns. Steinhauser (2000) emphasizes that biomedical aspects of care of the dying are crucial but merely provide a point of departure toward a good death. When all physical symptoms are properly assuaged, dying patients and their families need the opportunity to talk together at ease about their anxieties, fears and problems discussing also, psychosocial and spiritual matters with health professionals.

Death and Dying in the modern-day setting

In the hospital setting where the culture is too often focused on cure and lack of it regarded as failure, there is a reluctance to make the diagnosis of dying. Mills & Davies (1994) observed in their study in acute Scottish hospitals, that care of the dying was poor. They claimed that practical steps had to be implemented to facilitate high quality care of the dying. The authors also stated that much could be learned from the hospice movement and such knowledge and skills needed to be replicated in all settings.

Ellershaw (2003) advocates that expertise in the care of dying cancer patients needs to be disseminated widely and that it should include the non-cancer population. Core objectives related to the care of dying patients should be incorporated in the training of all medical and nursing students and all health care professionals (Pincombe & Brown, 2003; Toscani & Giulio, 2005; Ellershaw & Ward, 2003; Middlewood & Gardner, 2001). Indeed the standard of comprehensive care at the end of life should be an indicator of the performance of health systems.

Western society increasingly attributes near-miraculous powers to medical science- and increasingly avoids the subject of death. Many patients and physicians have come to regard the prolongation of life and the cure of disease as the fundamental and exclusive goals of modern medicine (Pan, 2008). Medical practitioners and medical institutions struggle daily to deal with individuals who cannot improve but who will die (Parker- Oliver 2000). There is a danger in modern hospitals to withdraw from the dying patient. This deficiency in traditional health care in the care of the dying, particularly in the acute hospital, may have many reasons. These include a tendency for the professional to withdraw from a dying person, from a sense of therapeutic frustration or inadequacy, a fear of failure, concerns about ones own mortality, inadequate understanding of pain and other symptoms or an over-emphasis on cure-oriented intervention associated with distressing side-effects (Parker- Oliver, 2000).

In Galenic tradition, physicians were trained to respect death's beckoning and allowed people at its threshold to step onto Charon's ferry. This was the threshold at which nature itself broke the healing contract held by the healer, a healer that respected and acknowledged his/her limits. At such a critical moment, withdrawal was the proper service a physician rendered to his patients in allowing a good death (Illich 1995). Unfortunately in many of today's hospitals there is a standard practice of withdrawal from a dying patient, which involves the very act of transferring the dying patient to a small side room removed from the regular ward round. It is at this moment that the hospice model of intensive palliative care, should come into action, into which friends and relatives may come, providing physical, psychological, social and spiritual care so to provide a comforting and comfortable death. (Ellershaw, 2003; Weinrich & Curtis, 2003).

These sentiments are reflected in the words of the American physician Alfred Worcester, when in his series of lectures, over 70 years ago, in 1935, noted "…many doctors nowadays, when the death of their patients become imminent, seem to believe that it is quite proper to leave the care of the dying in the care of the nurses and sorrowing relatives. This shifting of responsibility is unpardonable. One of its results is that as less professional interest is taken in such service less is known about it" (HHP, 2008). In this study on the moment of death, I aimed to listen and encourage the dying person and their relatives to share their experiences and needs at the moment of death, to approach them rather than to withdraw.

The Moment of Death

Kastenbaum (1999), states that the moment of death has been a symbolic reality for many years in many cultures. There is knowledge and wisdom to be gained by studying and reflecting on the positive aspects of care of the dying as practiced for hundreds of years by our ancestors (Donnelly, 1999 (a)). Donnelly (1999, (b)) has stated, that for too long dying has been to a large degree left un-described. Relatively few studies have focused on research of the dynamics of the death bed scene and a better understanding of dying is needed. (Kastenbaum 1999; Marwick 2003). Hence this study on the moment of death in a Specialist Palliative Care Unit aims to fulfill the need to examine this time for relatives of the dying and the dying themselves. Kastenbaum (1999) maintains that the moment of death inquiry should be useful in delineating core human values, fears and hopes which have become associated with the transition from life to death. All of life is encapsulated in that moment that brings both meaning and cessation. Clark (2003) ascribes to this view as he states that thus far our failure lies in not combining new ways of seeing death and dying by a method of research which draws explicitly on patients' perspectives, methods which would bring us back to the lost realization that death is central to life (Clark 2003). In accordance with the perspectives that my clinical experience as a doctor have taught me, this study on the moment of death aims to describe the last moments of the dying in a Specialist Palliative Care Unit, as recounted in interviews with bereaved relatives. Since there have been very few studies of this nature to date, this study is unique in how it captures the feelings, sentiments and wishes of the dying and their relatives as they share their last moments together.

Defining the moment of death in this study

The moment of death in this study is defined as the period surrounding the actual death of the person. This may include descriptions by relatives at interview of several hours before the death of their relative to exact minutes before death and the few hours after death. The time factor recounted depends on the relatives' presence in the room, however other relatives take over describing the scene if the other relative has left the room or has been away for the actual death. This study is one of three similar studies analyzing the moment of death, examining the moment of death in the home setting and in the acute hospital setting. This study (Donnelly, 2009 (a)) and the analysis of the moment of death in the home setting (Donnelly, 1996) have both been published and the study of the moment of death in the acute hospital setting is in print (Donnelly, 2009 (b)).

A 'Good Death'
The cultural model wherein palliative care has its roots refers to a style of good death which has its roots in Christian tradition of caring. The modern hospice can in fact be considered the belated fruit of the realisation of that process of 'caritas', which a follower of St Jerome started in Rome in the IV century A.D. (Toscani & Borreeni 2003). However despite a recent increase in the attention given to improving end of life care, our understanding of what constitutes a good death is surprisingly lacking (Steinhauser 2000). A good death has always been important in all cultures. To achieve your chosen afterlife you died either well (euthanatos) or nobly (kalosthanein) (Clark, 2003). In palliative care it is not only the quality of life that is important for the dying person but the concept of a 'good death' (Saunders ,2003). There is strong agreement that the concept of a good death is highly individual, changeable over time and based on the perspective and experience of both the dying person and professional carers. A 'good death' allows the patient to have a sense of control, of being comfortable, having a sense of closure, a sense of value and dignity, having trust in the carer, having the dying person's beliefs and values honoured and burdens minimized (Kehl 2006). Clark (2003) holds that patient's concepts of a good death should guide our efforts to make deaths better. Descriptions of a "good death" in modern Western culture are given by Clark (2002), as pain-free, with an open acknowledgement of the imminence of death, death at home surrounded by family and friends and an 'aware death', in which personal conflicts and unfinished business are resolved. Dyer (2006) outlines the principles of a good death as follows:

- To know when death is coming and to understand what can be expected
- To be able to retain control of what happens
- To be afforded dignity and privacy
- To have control over pain relief and other symptom control
- To have choice and control over where death occurs
- To have access to information and expertise of whatever kind is necessary
- To have access to any spiritual or emotional support required
- To have access to hospice care in any location
- To have control over who is present at death
- To have time to say goodbye and control over other aspects of timing.

Attempting to define what might be termed a "good death", Steinhauser (2000) and her colleagues gathered descriptions from seventy-five physicians, nurses, social workers, clergy members, patients, volunteers and bereaved families. Six major components of a good death were found:

Pain and Symptom Management: Many people fear dying in pain. Fear of pain and concerns about inadequate pain management can cause a significant amount of anxiety and distress for both the dying patient and their family.

Clear decision making: Patients feel more empowered when allowed to participate in decisions about treatment options. Patients want to have a say in their treatment plans. Fear of pain and concerns about poor symptom management can be reduced by good communication and determining a clear decision plan with the patient, their family and physicians. Clear plans discussed beforehand help reduce the chance of needing to make difficult decisions in the midst of a crisis.

Preparation for Death: Many patients want to know what to expect during the course of their illness. They want the opportunity to plan the events that follow their deaths- the will, the funeral, their obituary. Preparing for death may give patients a sense of completion, because the burden of planning these events does not fall on someone else.

Family members can prepare for the person dying by knowing the physical changes to expect when death arrives.

Completion: Includes finding meaningfulness at the end of life, which entails a personal review of life, resolving conflicts and spending time with family and friends. Issues of faith and ritual are also involved here and are an important part of the dying process and coping after death.

Contribution to others: Many people at the end of life have a desire to contribute to others. These contributions can be gifts, time or knowledge. As the end of a persons life draws nearer, many people finally discover what is important to them in life. They discover that personal relationships are more important than professional or monetary gains. Steinhauser (2000) quotes Dr Leo Buscaglia when he says:

Death teaches us……. that the time is now
Death teaches us the joy of the moment
It teaches us we don't have forever. Death says "Live now."

Affirmation of the whole person: It is important for health care providers to affirm or recognize the patient as a unique, whole person (with a mind, body and spirit). To consider the person in the context of their lives, their values and their personal preferences, not just a disease.

In this study, I demonstrate, how a 'good death' does occur in an institutional setting and indeed in Gott, Seymour & Clark's (2004) study, many participants identified a number of practical reasons against a choice for dying in their own home, such as, lack of an informal care, not wishing to be a 'burden' to their family, worries about material circumstances, the strain on the health of spouses, carers' or the transgression of the parent-child relationship. This does not of course negate the ideal and ultimate desire which the patient or family may have of dying and caring for the dying at home.

In a study of 40 different Italian hospitals, Toscani (2005), shows how dying patients, bereaved relatives, physicians and caregivers describe the three main features of a 'good death'; the dying person being kept clean, spending time with close friends and not dying alone. These qualities are exemplified in my findings from this study of the moment of death in a Palliative Care Unit. Saunders (2003) describes the principles of a 'good death' as the dying person being afforded dignity, privacy and having access to palliative care in any location, that of hospital, hospice or home. Lynn & Teno (1997) echo the sentiments of Steinhauser (2000) by stating that the death we fear most is dying in pain, unnoticed and isolated from loved ones.

In a study of the care of 50 dying patients in 4 large Scottish teaching hospitals by Mills & Davies (1994) care of many of the dying patients observed in these hospitals was poor. From this the authors concluded that we need to identify and implement practical steps to facilitate high quality care of the dying. Much can be learned from the hospice movement but such knowledge and skills must be replicated in all settings. The skills developed in hospices must be learnt in acute and general hospitals if the dying patients are to die with minimal discomfort (Mill & Davies, 1994).

Although the place of death ultimately must have much influence on how we die, Donnelly (2006) maintains that irrespective of the location of an anticipated death, the moment of death is so highly charged that it consequently needs to be handled skillfully by the professional carer. The author focuses on the moment of death in the home setting and clearly implies that a 'good death' is possible at home, in a hospice or hospital and regardless of the site the place of death is very important to family carers.

Valentine (2007), discusses a valid concept regarding the analysis of the moment of death with 25 families. The author refers to the juxtaposition of the profound and enduring sense of connection with the deceased with the more distressing aspects of the dying experience as leading to highly ambivalent constructions. I concur with Valentine (2007), as this study in a Palliative Care Unit demonstrates the contrast of the physical deterioration of the dying body and the surrounding distress with the peacefulness and beauty of the actual moment of death- "Although the final moment was easy and beautiful, it wasn't and easy death"- (Pat) - Valentine (2007).

My study on the moment of death echoes the above sentiments through the following direct quotes as provided by the grieving relatives of the dying patients in the study:

A relative describes her dying brother-in-law

"I felt the daytimes weren't too bad but the night times were desperate…….. I know he had difficulty breathing and it was kinda stressful looking at him, but you know the expression "you live as you die" … he gave only two gasps and he was gone… ..'twas his gentle nature, his serenity came through….. wasn't he beautiful."

Below a grieving husband describes his wife's death:

"She used to actually cry with that pain [in her hand]….. she was very frightened during the night. Her appetite went very fast, in the last week she ate nothing……. there were about ten in the room I thought she was unconscious the whole time but she knew there were people in the room but she never spoke. Never said a word. It was a very happy death."

According to Valentine (2007) the appreciation of the "ease" and "beauty" of these deaths was as much a function of their defeating as their redeeming aspects. By reflecting the vulnerability and frailty of the human condition they also affirmed the transcendental value placed on the unique individual life and the intimate relationships between individuals. These final moments represent the triumph of the human spirit over routine and impersonal medical settings. While Donnelly (2009) agrees with Valentine (2007) that dying moments in hospital were conveyed as social, memorable, dramatic and emotional events, Donnelly (2009 (b)) disagrees that individuals "demonstrated their freedom from the medicalised social order, "(Valentine 2007) but rather that relatives responded to the care, competence and compassion shown to them and the dying person by doctors, nurses, chaplains and care assistants. These qualities temporarily free relatives from their frustrations at the health system failures and communication inadequacies. I concur with Donnelly's (2009 (b)) viewpoint as demonstrated from my moment of death study, where relatives and patients respond with trust and appreciation to the compassion and professionalism of staff in the midst of their suffering and distress:

"[The staff] were marvellous to her, marvellous..... it was wonderful care."

"He was very well looked after.... they did everything that way to keep him comfortable. When we rang the bell they came straight away. They turned him, changed his clothes and washed him..... Sister Anne [Pastoral Care] she's been fantastic, you know she's like a mother."

"She seemed so happy here. We're still grateful for everything." I concur with Valentine (2008) where the author states that the narratives of those interviewed on the moment of death, reveals how "continuing bonds" with dead loved ones form a central part of grieving and serve not only the health and well-being of the living but also reflect the strength and enduring power of the social bond that continues beyond the life-death boundary.

Some Global Statistics relating to the Place of Death
In the Republic of Ireland, 30,000 people die each year of whom the majority wished to die at home (IHF, 2007), yet in fact two-thirds die in Irish hospitals. In a nationwide survey in the Republic of Ireland by the Irish Hospice Foundation (2004) entitled "Public Attitudes and Experiences regarding Death and Dying", See Table 3.1(a) & 3.1 (b). Among 1,000 adults asked for their preferred place of care when dying, 67% replied "in my own home", 10% chose a hospital and 10% chose a hospice. This pattern of stated preference differing significantly from the actuality emphasized by the CSO (2003), where 25% of all deaths in the Republic of Ireland were home deaths, 57.5%

occurred in a general, district or county hospital excluding deaths in private nursing homes and hospices.

Table 3.1 (a)

Preferred place of death Republic of Ireland, 2007

Total: 1000 patients

Home	67%
Hospital	10%
Hospice	10%

(Irish Hospice Foundation (IHF), 2004, 2007)

Table 3.1 (b)

Actual place of death Republic of Ireland

Total: 30,000 deaths in the year

General, district or county hospitals (excluding nursing homes and hospice)	57.5%
Home	25%

(CSO figures, Republic of Ireland, 2003)

The fact that these studies showing the home as the preferred place of death (IHF 2004; Townsend, Frank & Fermont, 1990; Fried, Van Doorn & O' Leary, 1999; Gott, Seymour & Bellamy, 2004), death in the hospital setting should not be demonized but rather should be subject as to how it can take on a more meaningful quality (Gott, 2004; Donnelly, 2006). These cold figures or statistics demonstrate not only that the wishes of the majority of Irish people are not being fulfilled in their preference for a place to die but that there is a great need for the provision of facilities and the training of multidisciplinary teams in relation to the care of the dying in the community and especially in the present acute hospital settings (Middlewood & Gardner, 2001). This is emphasized by Pincombe & Browne (2003), when they state that the implications for palliative care include the need to educate health care teams to plan and implement policy regarding the management of patients who are dying in the acute hospital setting.

Mills & Davies (1994), have stated that medical care in general hospitals concentrates on arresting disease and on recovery and rehabilitation. They claim that when death is inevitable palliative care must take priority over curative care. Since dying patients are an integral part of the population of general hospitals, their death should not be considered a failure since failure occurs only if a person's death is not as comfortable and dignified as possible.

In the majority of acute hospitals worldwide systems, attitudes and behaviours are designed to encourage the most efficient use of hospital resources and focus on the expectation of those patients' recovery. Pincombe & Browne (2003) concur with Mill & Davies (1994) in their Australian study of two acute care hospitals. Emphasizing this acute hospital tradition, Pincombe & Browne (2003) state that most acute care public hospitals operate on a curative model of health care and that care of the dying is neither a focus nor a priority of acute hospital activity. The authors conclude that since a high percentage of people die in the acute hospital setting, the appropriateness of their care should be addressed and strategies and procedural policies reviewed so that a palliative care approach can comfortably coexist with acute care in public hospitals. Since the majority of Irish people die in the acute hospital setting, (IHF, 2004; CSO, Republic of Ireland, 2003), See Table 3.1 (b), we can learn a lesson from these studies and make provisions for appropriate palliative care in our Irish acute hospitals.

From the beginning of their undergraduate training and through all their clinical training continuing through to postgraduate level medical and nursing students must be taught in the discipline of palliative medicine as part of their curriculum, a high standard of palliative care will be reached in the acute hospital, hospice and integrated with the home in the community settings providing people with the opportunity to die well, in the place of their choice. As Donnelly (2006) states that the painful, mysterious and intimate reality of dying needs to be given its place in the curriculum of palliative medicine training, as it already has its place in the community we serve. Many previous studies have found that the majority of cancer patients prefer to die at home (Tang, 2003; Tiernan, 2002; Dunlop, 1989). In the United Kingdom, See Table 3.2, figures too show that many patients would prefer to die at home (Higginson & Sen-Gupta, 2000; Townsend & Frank, 1990; Dunlop & Davies, 1989; Wilkes, 1984, Bowling, 1983; Willard & Luker, 2006), yet, only 20% achieve their wish. 54% die in the acute hospital setting, with a mere 4% in a hospice setting (Willard & Luker, 2006; Clark 1990). In the United States, See Table 3.3, two- thirds of adults die in hospitals and nursing homes, to the extent that many recent recommendations in the U.S. call for the expansion of the use of home and hospice as alternatives to hospital care (Fried & Van Doorn, 1999; Corr 1994; National Center for Health Statistics (NCHS), 2004).

In Australia, 90% of dying patients spend the majority of their final year at home with only 30% of those receiving palliative care services actually dying at home (PCA, 1999) State of the Nation 1998- Report of the National Census of Palliative Care Services. PCA, Canberra, 1999). The Commonwealth Government, in Australia has a commitment to improving patient access to palliative care, whether that be in the hospital, community or other setting.

Table 3.2

Comparison of place of death of patients in the United Kingdom and the United States.

UK, 2006

Place of death	%
Acute Hospital	20%
Home	54%
Hospice	4%

United Kingdom (Higginson, 2000; Dunlop, 1989; Wilkes, 1984; Bowling 1983; Clark 1990; Willard, 2006)

Table 3.3

U.S. 2004

Place of death	%
Acute hospital	46.11%
Home	24.4%
Nursing home/ long term care facility	22%
Other place	6.6%
Hospice	.43%
Unknown	.285%

United States (Fried, 1999; Corr,1994; National Center for Health Statistics, (NCHS), 2004)

In-patient hospice setting and 60% of South Australians surveyed replied that in the event of a terminal illness they would prefer to die at home. Despite this common but not universally expressed preference for home, the actual place of death is most likely to be a large hospital (Middlewood & Gardner, 2001). See Table 3.4 for the comparison of percentages of place of deaths in South Australia and

New South Wales (Bachelor Report, 2009; Cancer Institute NSW, 2007).

The Medicalization or Institutionalisation of Dying

The medicalization of death and dying similar to medical and nursing withdrawal from the dying patient is another contemporary phenomenon present and increasing under the influence of medical technology (Burgess, 1993). Much of the literature and research concerning the modern attitude to death contains a pervasive theme, which is a critique of hospitalized, medicalized death and its representation as a threat to an idealized 'good' death (Seymour, 2001). Medicalized death is described as divorced from lay

Table 3.4

Place of Death, of cancer patients South Australia and New South Wales, 1990-2003

	Place of Death Cancer patients South Australia 1990-1999	Place of Death of Cancer patients New South Wales, Australia 1989-2003
Public Hospitals	25%	41%
Private hospitals	12.7%	6.2%
Country hospitals	16.9%	17.2%
Home	15.8%	16.9%
Nursing homes	9.7%	8.8%

(Bachelor Report, 2009)
(Cancer Institute NSW, 2007)

I would rather use the phrase institutionalization of death and dying as opposed to medicalization of death and dying as an appropriate critical description of the negative aspects of dying in hospital, where the latter implies an onslaught of medical care as a negative aspect of dying where medicine heretofore has been therapeutic and healing in nature. The term medicalization is not used when describing the care of the dying at home, where there is very little use of tubes and drains, machines and needles, yet therapeutic medical care is at its centre. The mere presence of the patient and relatives in a hospital building shows that institutionalization brings with it the machines the tubes and the persistant interventions particular to the acute hospital setting. The Ars Moriendi, a body of Christian literature detailing the craft of dying, where dying was constructed as such a key transition in a person's life (Aries, 1981; Bell, 2005). It instructed the dying person to make the following preparations: examine ones life, seek God's forgiveness, forgive others, declare ones faith, place oneself into God's hands and ensure that ones family was provided for both spiritually and materially. The deathbed scene with family and friends formed an important social occasion.

The occasion was characterized by highly charged moments in which every word, deed, expression and gesture assumed meaning (Cressy, 1997). Kastenbaum (1999) has observed, that this once dominant concept has become destabilized by medical and technological advances and consequent changes in clinical practice. These have made it much more difficult to assume any actual definable moment of transition. Alongside this, the dominant religious, philosophical and scientific beliefs that supported the traditional death-bed scene have been increasingly questioned and marginalized. I concur with Valentine (2007), who in a previous study on the moment of death, involving interviews of 25 bereaved relatives in England, demonstrates how in a medicalized context, which emphasizes the biological nature of dying, these dying moments represent gestures of leave-taking in which elements lost to the medical discourse, but vital to making sense of mortality, were recovered: the spiritual, humanistic, social and emotional aspects of the dying experience. This study on the moment of death in a Specialist Palliative Care Unit in the Mid-West of Ireland demonstrates the presence of nature, expressed in the Irish language, as 'an nadúr', at the dying persons bedside and the natural art of the community and staff in the care of the dying, coming from generations past in Irish culture, it shows compassion and love, through dignity, vigil, faith and religious beliefs. Ritual, mutual self-giving, mutual respect and complete attention is given to mind, soul and body of the dying person at the deathbed. Valentine's (2007) study on the moment of death reveals the limitations of medical discourse and the perception of death as a failure. The authors account is similar to my moment of death study in that dying moments were conveyed as sacred, memorable, dramatic and emotional events. Continuing bonds were forged between bereaved people and their deceased loved ones. These bonds affirmed the transcendental value placed on the unique individual life and the intimate relationships between individuals. Valentine's (2007) moment of death narratives convey the triumph of the human spirit over the depersonalizing nature of biological dying. From its origin, in the art of healing the sick and wounded, medicine has grown into a technologically oriented science, a science which increasingly penetrates our daily lives. No longer is death a 'natural' occurrence. Death though omnipresent in the practice of medicine, has no well understood place in medical theory. The relentless "specialization" and "technologization" of medicine undermines the therapeutic importance of recognizing patients in the context of their lives and of bearing witness to their suffering (Charon, 2001). According to Middlewood & Gardner (2001), a common theme of North American literature on death and dying, is that dying patients receive inadequate and inappropriate care in the acute hospital setting because their needs do not fit with the ideology of large hospitals, where the main purpose of care is to cure using increasingly sophisticated interventions.

Clark (2002) states how palliative care has encouraged medicine to be gentler in its acceptance of death, yet medical services in general continue to regard death as something to be resisted, postponed or avoided. Kubler-Ross (1997) asks, in a changing field of medicine, whether medicine is to remain a humanitarian and respected profession or a new and depersonalized science in the service of prolonging life rather than diminishing human suffering.

Illich (1976) argues that modern medicine constitutes an epidemic of cultural iatrogenesis in that it undermines the ability of individuals to face their reality, to express their own values and to accept inevitable and often irremediable pain, impairment, decline and eventual death. Illich considers that a society's image of death reveals the level of independence of its people, their personal relatedness, selfreliance and aliveness (Illich, 1995). Unconsciously or not, death is not construed as an inevitable biological denouement but as a medical failure. Death has been moved out of nature into the realm of human responsibility. We have made mortality itself our fault, our responsibility (Callahan, 1993; Pan 2008). The art of Palliative medicine does not view death and dying as a failure but introduces and fulfills what is lacking in the medicalisation of care of the dying as it seeks to serve both patient and family in the dying process (Parker-Oliver, 2000). Palliative medicine focuses not only on pain control and symptom management, but also provides care in a holistic, individualistic manner, encompassing the emotional, psychological and spiritual aspects of the person by an interdisciplinary team of professionals. The single goal is not to prolong life, but to enhance its quality and help individuals renegotiate meaning and purpose by redefining their lives, not in terms of being 'sick', but in terms of living until they die (Parker-Oliver, 2000). Palliative medicine does not see patients as merely malfunctioning lungs or defective kidneys. They are living persons, a fact which is sometimes missed in contemporary medicine. A distinguishing feature of palliative care is that it openly acknowledges dying as part of living and does not consider death as the enemy (Pan, 2008).

Byock (2002) states that as a clinician it seems disrespectful to discuss the "meaning and value" of death. In the rightful regard for the preciousness of life which underlies all clinical disciplines the preservation of life should become the only and paramount clinical goal. For clinicians, death is the enemy to be conquered and when it occurs it represents defeat, failure. As the 17th century French writer and moralist, La Rochefoucauld reminds us "One can no more look steadily at death than at the sun" (Byock, 2002). In looking steadily at death, we as professionals find it very difficult to stand by and watch. The art of palliative medicine is in knowing when to act and intervene and when to stand by.

Physicians and nurses cannot guarantee that all symptoms will be fully controlled, nor that every person will die well. However clinicians can commit to doing whatever is necessary to alleviate physical and mental distress. Physicians can commit to not giving up, to never abandoning patients and to being present for them and their families. This is the ground substance for human responsiveness. We have the capacity to bear witness to patients and their relatives which offers the potential for strengthening relationships between individuals that are of profound value to the people involved (Byock, 2002).

In our past culture death was accepted and not feared. Death was as natural as breathing. The faith of the people and their belief in the spiritual world allowed death to be a natural extension of life. There were no aggressive measures, no desperate attempts to prolong life. The dying person simply moved from one form of existence to another (Donnelly, 1999 (a)). We need to learn from our past. By recognizing its wisdom we can use it in our care of the dying to-day. There is a danger in our expertise and professionalism of disempowering the dying person and their natural carers, of sidelining the foundation of their relationship, that is love (Donnelly, 1999 (a)).

What emerges from this study on the moment of death in a Palliative Care Unit, is a verity that love is the foundation of the care of the dying, by family and professional carers alike. This is emphasized by Byock (2002) when he states that, love is not only stronger than death but that love affirms life in the face of death. Byock (2o02) concludes that the confrontation with death, lays bare the spiritual core of the human condition which rises up in response to the awe-inspiring and terrifying mystery of life and the universe.

Research

Cassaret (2002) records that that there is a dramatic increase in research that involves dying patients and that hospices are increasingly becoming involved in research. At the same time Lynn& Teno (1997) remind us that little research to date has focused on describing or improving the experience of dying. They conclude that except for data on mortality rates, the medical literature includes little information about dying. Without doubt as Kendall (2007) states, there are continuing taboos around death and dying and these act as a barrier to the commissioning and conduct of end of life research. The author reiterates that some people facing death, may want to participate in research and should be allowed to do so. Ethics committees and clinical staff, however, must balance understandable concern about non-maleficence with the wishes and rights of people with advanced illness to participate in research. As long ago as 40 years ago, Kubler-Ross (1969) a pioneer in research with dying patients describes her initial difficulties in interviewing dying patients in the acute hospital setting:

"…….. I set out to ask physicians of different services and wards for permission to interview their terminally ill patients. The reactions were varied from stunned looks of disbelief to abrupt changes of topic of conversation, the end result being not interviewing a single patient. Others bluntly refused to take part in such a project. Doctors were both very defensive when it came to talking about death and dying. My phone calls and personal visits to the wards were [initially] all in vain…….. however when I finally met my first dying patient he welcomed me with open arms."

Such findings broadly agree with Feifel (1959) studies where he tells us that persistence led to the finding that many dying patients were grateful for the opportunity to talk about their situation. In their contemporary study of hospice patients views on research in palliative care, Olsen & Ravenscroft (2006) found, that the total of 22 patients admitted to the hospice wished to participate in the research and stated that they wanted to help others through their participation and expressed how they valued the commitment by doctors to optimizing palliative care by research. This is confirmed and reflected in my study on the moment of death in which relatives and patients expressed to me their willingness to participate and their sense of obligation to contribute to the care and the needs of future patients. After-death interviews with bereaved respondents, as in this study, are an important tool in the repertoire of researchers evaluating the quality of end-of-life care or investigating the experiences of people at the end of life (Addington-Hall & McPherson, 2001). At the same time the authors claim that despite the importance of after-death interviews to our understanding of the last months of life, the validity of the information has received little attention to-date.

This study on the moment of death listens to and expresses the concerns and needs of dying patients and their relatives at this significant time. Lynn & Teno (1997), remind us that dying is not only what the patient experiences but also what the family remembers. This reflects Dame Cicely Saunders a pioneer in the hospice movement in England, when she stated "how people die remains in the memories of those who live on" (Saunders, 1989). The importance of discovering the experiences not only of the dying patient but also family relatives cannot be over-estimated. We, as professionals and medical doctors, must learn not only how to provide a good death for those who are dying but also to help to create memories of a good death for those who are living. It is the memory of death and how the patient died that will live on with the relatives and which will have an influence for good on their adjustment to bereavement and indeed on their subsequent health (Addington-Hall & McPherson, 2001). We who have witnessed the dying and death of a relative and their experience of a good death can echo the words of Ira Byock (1997) "when the human dimension of dying is nurtured, for many the transition from life can be so profound, intimate and precious as the miracle of birth."

Valentine's (2007) study on the experience of the moment of death of patients through interviews with 25 bereaved individuals in England, considers the sociological significance of dying moments as gestures of leave taking, noting how this was a function of the relationship between the dying person and his or her loved one. What transformed dying moments into significant personal and social events was their reciprocal and shared nature (Donnelly, 2006; Kellehear & Lewin, 1988- 1989).

This reciprocity is very much evident in this study on the moment of death in a Palliative Care Unit, where mutual accompaniment at the death bed involves both patient and relative, where gestures of love are given through touching and embracing, by communication through facial expressions and sounds and also the simple act by the dying person of waiting for a travelling relative to reach the bedside. Mutual giving is strongly present as part of leave taking and the final acts of farewell.

According to Kellehear & Lewin (1988-1989), in their study of 100 Australian dying patients, at the most practical and interpersonal level, farewells tend to be times for the exchange of affection, reassurance and acceptance with these interactions supplying reaffirmation and support to both patient and family with many patients mentioning that merely to have their loved ones at the bedside would be a comfort and the goodbye would be embodied in looks and gestures rather than words. The authors conclude that farewells are an important way of reaffirming social bonds, of making dying a socially real and shared experience and of helping people to disengage. Valentine (2007) reaffirms this by stating that these gestures of intimacy and relatedness signaled the dying persons imminent leave taking.

On the topic of qualitative research with dying patients, Kellehear (1989) cautions us against the arrogance of assuming that comfort and safety, as important as they are, are more important to dying patients than their desire to be heard or their desire to contribute. This is supported by Clark (2003) when he calls for more qualitative research involving patients and families, cross cultural research, longitudinal studies that can identify the changing needs of both patients and families and the use of innovative methods to examine the difficulties of research in palliative care settings.

Proot & Abu-Saad (2004) caution that while the needs assessment of dying people constitutes an important part of palliative care and that although previous studies have delivered important insights into the physical, psychosocial, existential and spiritual needs of dying patients, the authors maintain that some of these studies have a number of limitations; they do not address the needs of the patients at different stages of the dying process and in different settings such as hospital, home and hospice.

Kastenbaum (1999) defines the ethical principle, that no palliative care program should compromise the welfare of its clients by intrusive research procedures and that firm ethical guidelines must be adhered to. The author emphasises that any palliative care provider who is observant of patient and family and the meaning associated with the moment of death and the death bed scene, can provide affirmation in the face of despair. Without the guidance that research gives, the dying have no idea how others like them die and they want to know; when we become them we may want to know too (Kellehear, 1989). The same author also reminds us, at the same time, that we as researchers are responsible for any effect of our intrusion and have the responsibility to minimize any disturbance of the participants it may cause. A balance must be achieved between early interview of relatives after death and ethical concerns about upsetting people too soon after death (Addington- Hall & McPherson, 2001). In reiterating this, by stating that end of life research can be conducted with ethical and methodological rigor, Kendall (2007) adds the proviso that adequate psychological support must be provided for participants. The biggest challenge to-day for researchers and for all methods of research in palliative medicine in valuing the dying person and his or her relatives, is how to nurture, support and affirm meaning as the moment of death approaches. As health professionals we should take our cues from patients and their families for all methods of research in palliative medicine, rather than imposing predetermined sets of values and procedures (Kastenbaum, 1999). In this study on the moment of death, I adhere to these strict ethical guidelines at all times as detailed in the explanation of the study in Chapter 6.

Chapter 4.
Death and Dying: Ethical Approaches

Defining "Ethics"

Ethics can be viewed as the science of morals, a system of rules of behaviour (MacDonald, 1972), and defined as the examination of the nature of moral life, the study of right and wrong and an attempt to systematise and explain the nature of good and evil. These definitions emphasise its rationalising and organising intent and the search for universally-applied codes. The field of ethics is a vast academic discipline. It is the pursuit of what is good and right from the outside. If ethics can be regarded as the pursuit of the grand narrative of good and bad, morality is the pursuit of good and bad in multiple, individualised, personal narratives in which each person tries to respond to a call to the good and understand what it means to be good through a lifetime of individual acts and self-reflection. Morality returns ethics to the personal (Bauman, 1993)

Ethics in Palliative Medicine

Palliative medicine constitutes such a moral arena, an arena in which ethics is personalised and its research as in all research, we have to be fully aware and observant of our effects on participants. In this study on the moment of death, I ask is my involvement as researcher in the dying patients and relatives' lives too invasive and whether the interviews with relatives one week after death ethical? In a study based in an Academic Palliative Medical Unit in Sheffield, England, by Stevens, Wilde & Paz (2003), on a review of palliative care research protocols in England, Wales and Scotland, revealed that most ethical concerns were dependant on the following:

How qualitative research is carried out, especially the protection of patients.

The influence and input of the researcher in the process.

The impact of the research on the participant, particularly intrusion and potential distress.

In accordance with Kastenbaum (1999) when he states, that no palliative care program should compromise the welfare of its patients by intrusive research procedures, these factors were considered carefully and applied with rigour in this study on the moment of death. As will be explained in Chapter 6, full explanations were given at the beginning of this study and confidentiality assured to participants. Both patients and relatives were allowed to participate of their own free-will and to withdraw from the study at any time. My influence as researcher in the study was kept to a minimum, from my first meeting with relatives and patients where I encouraged them to speak at length of their needs and feelings at the time with no interruption from me.

Patients and relatives were also enthusiastic about being part of the study and were eager to express their needs and concerns to me as a researcher and on its completion relatives expressed relief and appreciation at having the opportunity to talk at the interviews.

For this enquiry into the moment of death in a Specialist Palliative Care Unit, I obtained ethical approval from the Mid- West Ethics and Research Committee. See Appendix 8.1.

Ethics in Qualitative Research
Qualitative research with in-depth interviews can be safely and ethically conducted with bereaved families, if performed sensitively according to Hynson & Aroni (2006). Their study examined the impact of qualitative interview research process on bereaved parents and which elements enhanced the experience of research participation. Their findings concur with my own where during my study there was no evidence of distress or disturbance in my relationship as researcher with the dying patients and their families, only a welcoming and trusting one. Hynson & Aroni (2006) found that although the majority of parents chose to participate in the in-

depth interviews for altruistic reasons, many described the research process through interview as personally beneficial.

This was confirmed in my interviews also, where there were no signs of stress or disturbance among patients or relatives, as evidenced by the trusting relationship between myself and the dying patient and their relatives. De Raeve (1994) counteracts the above by stating that no research is morally justifiable with the dying as participants and that no research methodology is benign. My experience leads me to reject this statement as unjustifiably extreme and would not consider this qualitative enquiry unethical or damaging to participants, on the contrary, as was previously discussed, participants communicated with me how they found the interviews of help to them in their grief. I adopted Kellehear's (1989) ethical approach to research by emphasising empathy and interpersonal sensitivity as critical. I obtained verbal consent at the initial stages of the study from both patient and relative and written consent from relatives prior to the interviews. At such a sensitive time in the families grief, the empathy and consideration required to obtain family consent for interviews in this study, necessitated considerable time and effort (Rinck, 1997; Ross & Cornbleet, 2003). This effort required the regular and frequent visiting and meeting with family relatives and dying patients each day for several weeks or months prior to the death of the patient and the posthumous interviews with relatives.

After-death interviews with relatives in this study
Addington-Hall (2001) reminds us that after death interviews with bereaved respondents form an important tool in the repertoire of researchers, evaluating the quality of end of life care. Also important, for the full validity of the research is the pre and post death experience and the recollection, a period crucial to the accuracy of the recalled information and the ease to which it is recalled by the family mourners (Bradley 1990). The short interval in my study of 8 days, on average 22 days, with a range of 8-42 days, between the death of the patient and interview with relatives, is innovative compared with that of previous studies involving intervals extending to 2years

(Cartwright & Seale 1990; Higgonson, Priest & McCarthy, 1994; Hinton, 1996; Ahmedazai & Morton, 1998; Stroebe & Schut, 2003. Addington-Hall (2001) concludes that the use of family members in obtaining information as surrogates for dying patients is valid. However, the author also states that after-death interviews must balance against the possible ethical transgressions of intrusion so soon after death, recognizing the family time of mourning and the awareness of the accuracy of recall, particularly the concerns about bothering bereaved people too soon after death. Of this I as fully aware in designing and undertaking the interviews for this study and I never pressurized relatives in any way. I would have ended the interview immediately if there was any evidence of distress. This situation never arose in at any stage of this study.

Mindful of the sensitivity of the topic (Addington – Hall & McPhearson, 2001; Stroebe, Stroebe & Schut, 2003) emphasis was placed on minimising potential distress to the families and at all times being tactful and considerate. Meeting family members prior to the patient's death facilitated the early postbereavement visit. Due to the families prior acceptance of the presence of professional carers in the care of their dying relative in the Specialist Palliative Care Unit, each family member were very open and willing to talk with and trust in me, as researcher. There is no doubt that this fact assisted in the close and trusting relationship between myself as a doctor and researcher and the families throughout the study. This relationship of confidence and trust not only enriched the data obtained but in itself and the surcease it afforded, emphasized as it enhanced its positive ethical aspects.

The ethical dilemma of involving dying patients in research The continuing taboos around death and dying, which show global variations, act as barriers to the commissioning and conduct of end of life research. Nevertheless, some people facing death may want and wish to participate in research and should be allowed to do so. McLoughlin (1992) states in concurrence with Siber (1992) that those participating in qualitative research, feel it gives them an opportunity to reflect on a significant life event and they may come to value the time spent with the researcher. Despite the inherent difficulties, end of life research can be conducted with ethical and methodological rigour. The universal medical ethos of doing no harm is important especially when palliative care patients are involved in research (Jarret 1999). As reflected in this qualitative enquiry, I agree with McLoughlin (2002) who states that it is only by involving, asking and listening to such patients about their care that any improvements regarding future care can be made.

Chochinov (2009) reminds us of the infamous Palliative Medical physician Dr Eduardo Bruera who when asked

"Was it right to ask palliative care patients near the end of life, to expend effort in answering our research questions?" He answered simply, that were we convinced that the quality of care, the efficacy of treatment and the completeness of knowledge underpinning palliative care were beyond reproach or the possibility of improvement? If so, there was neither justification nor cause to proceed with research. On the other hand, if care for the dying is less than optimal-whether in reference to the physical, psychological, psychosocial, spiritual or existential challenges facing patients and families confronting life-threatening or life-limiting conditions- how can we morally justify not doing palliative care research (Chochinov, 2009).

Below is a response to evidence albeit anecdotal, that the Human Research Ethics Committee (UK), has real concern that dying patients are involved in research because of their vulnerability, which can be found in the summary of Lee & Kristjanson (2003).

"The suggestion that palliative care patients should not be involved in research denies these individuals an active role in living and prevents them from contributing to knowledge about how to improve care for others…they have the right to choose to participate in an activity that may bring benefit to others, particularly when the research they choose to be involved in has little risk of harm to them. Participation in research projects by palliative care patients can bring forward a number of extremely positive opportunities. These include an opportunity for patients to reflect upon their care and illness experience, a sense of contributing to a greater community good and a feeling of pride in being able to offer information that may benefit others."

Despite this, according to the American Academy of Hospice and Palliative Medicine Statement, (AAHPM) (2007), debate still exists on whether patients near the end of life should ever be asked to participate in research. Consequently, some clinicians, ethics committees and investigators remain uncertain about the ethical limits of research involving dying patients and their families. However, the Academy believes that there is an urgent need for further palliative care research that will

(a) increase overall knowledge in the field.

(b) provide evidence to define the standard of care.

(c) increase access to high quality care.

These elements are not unique to palliative care research but they deserve emphasis because of the unique vulnerability of this patient population.

The American Academy of Hospice and Palliative Medicine (AAHPM, 2007) recommendations accord with the qualitative research undertaken in this study in a Specialist Palliative Care Unit, where I have aimed to achieve ethical standards particularly in the area of ensuring sensitivity to participants at all times:

Minimisation of incremental risks: Always attempt to minimize a study's incremental risk. Incremental risk is the amount of additional risk due to study participation above and beyond the known risks of standard treatment.

Minimisation of burdens: Due to the frequency of malaise, energy limitations and potentially limited life-span, investigators should justify the importance of each survey, interview and/or study visit. Investigators should also minimize the burdens that a study for friends and family members as well as patients. Minimization of distress: The risks of causing distress, especially in interview studies, are very small and may be balanced by the benefits that subjects receive (such as, a chance to talk about difficult issues). Limited research indicates that the risk of self reported distress from participation in palliative care research is usually small. Survey questions ought to be worded sensitively to further minimize and cause of distress.

Decision-making capacity: Patients who consent to participate in research should have adequate decision making capacity. This includes the patients' ability to understand relevant information, appreciate the significance of that information and reason through to a conclusion that makes sense to them.

While there is no inherent reason why patients who are… receiving palliative care are less able to make informed decisions about whether or not to participate in research according to Cassaret & Karlawish (2000), I concur with Keeley (2008) who states that the following arguments should be highlighted to justify the need for effectiveness research in palliative care.

1. There is evidence of an untapped altruism amongst the population of palliative care patients who would be keen to be involved in such research.

Traditional virtue ethics would point to the need to gain knowledge in and of itself, but especially in palliative medicine for the benefit of patients. A stock of research experience in turn makes further research feasible.

Jubb (2002) asserts that the potential of palliative medical research is still held back by a paucity of good evidence. These circumstances are largely attributable to perceived ethical challenges that allegedly distinguish dying patients as a special client class. In addition practical limitations compromise the quality of evidence that can be obtained from empirical research on dying patients. Jubb (2002), concludes that provided investigators compassionately apply ethical principles to their work, there is no justification for not endeavouring to improve the quality of palliative care through research.

The field of palliative care depends on rigorous research to guide clinical care. Vulnerable patients and families can be protected and research can proceed by ensuring optimal study design, by minimizing risks, burdens and distress, by ensuring a careful informed consent process and by recruiting subjects from an environment with excellent standards of palliative care. (Jubb, 2002).

At the beginning of the study a letter of explanation was given to both patients and relatives See Appendix 8.2. This letter did not mention about the interviews that were to take place with relatives after the death of the patient. The issue of the interview was explained privately to the relatives at a later stage and verbal consent obtained. Written consent was obtained for the interviews from the relatives on the day of the interview, See Appendix 8.3. Strict confidentiality was assured at all times. More details are given on this topic in Chapter 6. The National Health and Medical Research Council (UK) state in their National Statement (1999), that researchers will need to demonstrate that inclusion in the research is not contrary to the participants interests and that the research poses no greater risk to the participant than is inherent in their condition or treatment.

In this study on the moment of death, I attempted to weigh up the potential benefits against any potential risks or harm to participants. Although most frequently understood in physical terms, "harm" can also encompass psychological distress, discomfort, social disadvantage, invasion of privacy and infringement of rights. I considered all these issues when performing this study and ensured no harm would come in any way to either patients or relatives.

The premise that a palliative care patient is in a vulnerable position and can be exploited can further cloud the issues surrounding informed consent. Vulnerability of the patient can express itself in a number of ways:

A compulsion to participate in research out of a sense of desperation makes the patient willing to try anything in the hope that they will benefit.

An obligation to participate due to a feeling of dependency on the researcher.

Feeling the need to 'give something back' to show gratitude for care received.

A reduction in decision-making capacity.

An inability to concentrate for sufficiently long periods of time prevents full understanding of the information relevant to a particular study.

The presence of cognitive impairment.

(Casarett & Karlawish, 2000; Rees, 2001; Jubb 2002.)

These issues between desperation and obligation to be involved in palliative care research are relevant to all clinical research but do not constitute a specific arguement against palliative care research (Karim 2000). As I showed previously, relatives and patients wished and indeed were enthusiastic to be included in the study and expressed eagerness to help in any way so that others might benefit.

In balancing the role of clinician and researcher, there are two main scenarios in which ethical issues may arise.

The researcher is independent from the care giving process

The researcher is a clinician involved in the care of research participants.

Both a practical and an ethical issue arises when the researcher obtains information of potential significance for the present clinical management of a patient which information is not given or available to those caring for the patient. There are three options available to the researcher:

Never divulge information to the patient's professional carers out of a duty to maintain confidentiality and to ensure that patients give complete and accurate information on the basis that any breach of confidentiality might jeopardise the validity of the research.

Disclose all clinically important information thereby ensuring the maximum of benefit and minimal of harm of the research. Compromise by taking a middle ground between those two extremes or decide that the researcher should not contact the professional carer without the patients consent or that of the nearest responsible carer should the patients clinical state prevent speech or communication. Alternatively, the researcher should recommend that the patient or the nearest relative as indicated, tell the patients doctor. This recognises the fundamental right of patients to make informed decisions about their treatment, and preserves the confidentiality of information divulged. It also meets the obligation of researchers to engage in ethical conduct. According to the Ethical Research guide in Palliative Care by the Human Research Ethics Committee (UK) (2003), the third option is most recommended.

As the researcher in this study on the moment of death I chose the second option. I as doctor and researcher had to discern how to separate both roles. I was ready to distinguish between information divulged to me as a researcher applicable to my study and any clinical information given to me that I interpreted as a doctor. Any information that a patient or relative might have revealed to me regarding their situation I recommended they tell the doctor, nurse, social worker or Pastoral Care teams tending to them.

As the study progressed the only information I disclosed to the professional care team for the welfare of the patient or relative was where a relative expressed the need or wished to talk further about their grief. I recommended that the relative speak further with a bereavement counsellor on the social work team and contacted the team on their behalf.

Chapter 5:
Moment of Death:
The Role of Spirituality in Palliative Care

Over the last twenty years both within palliative care and within health care in general, research related to spirituality and health has developed from relative obscurity to a thriving field of study (Sinclair & Pereira, 2006). Attention to psychosocial-spiritual needs is considered critical by patients with life-threatening illnesses and their caregivers. Traditionally, the moment of death was constructed as a crucial preparation for the after-life and invested with profound personal, social and religious significance (Valentine, 2007). Thus life and death were inextricably linked, and most crucially by means of a persons dying moments. Dying was constructed as such a key transition in a persons life that a craft of dying was developed and enshrined in a body of Christian literature, the Ars Moriendi (Aries, 1981; Bell, 2005; Cressy, 1997). In the 14th and 15th Centuries, such texts were widely disseminated to provide detailed instructions for the benefit of both the dying and their helpers on the best way to prepare oneself for what was perceived as the moment of destiny when the soul would be released to its fate (O'Connor, 1966; Houlbrooke, 1998).

In Irish culture, care of the dying was inextricably linked to their faith for generations. There was no need for written texts to teach them how to care for their dying. A sense of community and accompanying rituals were handed down. Many of these rituals are revealed in this study as a natural process. The only rehearsal for death was the way life had been lived and the love shared with their families. Generations of their families before them had lived their faith and as in this study even if their faith wasn't practiced during life, at the death bed their faith reveals itself once more.

"[The ritual, the prayer] it's a comfort to the person that's dying……."

"I'd say she was awake. Bernadette knew everything that was happening, even though she wasn't talking. The one thing she really enjoyed was the rosary….. she was a fierce holy woman. She was a very religious woman…. you'd know when you'd say the rosary, the smile would come on her face… she really enjoyed it….."

"There was a little cross on the tray and then he had his own that we brought in and a candle. Sister had a prayer book and we said the prayers…"

"Thomas had a lot of prayers and he said to me that he was eventually saying two rosaries a day. When he wasn't able to say them I'd try to say them…. but he had a lot of prayers."

Hills & Paice (2005) state that one's spirituality or religious beliefs and practices may have a profound impact on how individuals cope with suffering that so often accompanies advanced disease. Millar & Chibnall (2005), hold that palliative care interventions which address these needs, particularly the spiritual, have been lacking, while Marr & Billings (2007) support the view that spirituality still remains a major domain within palliative medicine. Throughout this study, which I undertook in a Specialist Palliative Care Unit, I noted the sense of spirituality that permeated the study, through the professional carers, the families and friends but mostly through the dying patients. One of the most critical aspects of dealing with life threatening or death certain illness is the desire among patients to "live well until they die", to prepare for death, psychologically, emotionally and spiritually (Millar & Chibnall, 2005). Most if not all models of comprehensive palliation, stress the importance of spirituality as an integral factor in caring for patients, family and staff (Purdy, 2002; Chochinov, 2005).

Spirituality which has been recognized as the core or essence of a person and as an essential part of an individuals wellbeing and is not to be confused with religiosity, a narrower concept than spirituality and refers to organized religion with codified belief systems, whereas spirituality neither has the codification nor the organization (Clark & Leady, 2007; Chochinov, 2005).

In providing care for the dying, there must be a high quality palliative care service to enhance the quality of life for all patients and their families. This is achieved by providing holistic care including the physical, psychological, spiritual and emotional wellbeing of all dying patients (Chochinov, 2006). The American Institute of Medicine identify several domains of quality end-of-life care in their 1997 report (Field & Cassel, 1997). These include:

1. Overall quality of life,

2. Physical well-being and functioning,

3. Achieving a sense of spiritual peace and well-being,

4. Patient perception of care

5. Family wellbeing and functioning.

Dying, the one true certainty of life, should be as natural an experience as birth. It should be a meaningful experience for the dying person, a time when the dying find meaning in their suffering Puchalski (2002). As Victor Frankl (1984) wrote "man is not destroyed by suffering, he is destroyed by suffering without meaning". In to-day's society, suffering has lost its meaning. As society contributes to our denial of death, so religion loses many of its believers in life after death (Kubler- Ross, 1997).

Denial of the religious belief in the meaning of suffering here on earth has not offered hope and purpose but has only increased our anxiety and contributed to our destructiveness and aggressiveness (Kubler-Ross, 1997). In our care of the dying we need to address the spiritual aspect of the dying patient. This can involve simply listening, conversing, laughing, embracing, praying with, being present with and to the dying person (Chochinov, 2005).

It is our responsibility as doctors and palliative care professionals, to listen to dying people's anxieties and fears, their wishes, hopes, regrets and despairs. The serenity which comes with acceptance can also be generated through faith and spirituality, promoting healing, not necessarily of a physical kind but in the restoration of a sense of self, of a sense of wholeness and in ones relationship with others (Puchalski, 2002). In the growing realization that while spirituality and religion can affect every aspect of an individuals life, individuals at a time of suffering near death, struggle frequently with fear, anger, physical discomfort, loss of independence, troubling spiritual questions, changing self-images, roles and relationships. At these times a patients spirituality and religious beliefs and practices can have a profound positive impact on how they cope with these issues (Hill & Paice, 2005; Chochinov, 2005; Koenig, 2001).

Part of getting to know the dying person is to ascertain gently and slowly a spiritual history taken by the doctor as part of a detailed medical and clinical history, acknowledging the spiritual aspect of care of the dying person. As with all aspects of palliative care it must be patient centred, where respect for the patient's wishes is given at all times and personal and appropriate boundaries are maintained. This respect for patient's privacy, including matters of spirituality and religion must be upheld and physicians and health care providers should avoid imposing their own beliefs on the patient (Puchalski 2002). Spirituality in its widest sense embraces many aspects of human behaviour and expresses itself in the presence of the dying. It is as important for healthcare providers to talk with patients about spiritual issues as it is to address the medical and practical side of care (Puchalski 2002). Spirituality is central to the dying person and is well recognized by many experts, the most of whom are our patients (Puchalski, 2002). In a survey by Gallup (1997) of a representative sample of 1,200 Americans, over half wanted to reclaim and reassert the spiritual dimensions in dying. A third of respondents stated that if they were dying, having a doctor who was spiritually atuned to them would be very important. Overall respondents wanted warm relationships with their carers, to be listened to, to have someone with them when they are dying, to be able to pray, to have others pray with them and to have a chance to say goodbye to family and friends. When asked what would worry them most, they said not being forgiven by God or by others and to have continued emotional and spiritual suffering. In this study on the moment of death in a Palliative Care Unit, the relationship between the spiritual and its benefits to both families and the dying person were observed not only by the expression of faith through prayer and ritual by the bedside, such as lighted candles, holy water, rosary and crucifix, but in the expressions of love and affection, a human and at the same time spiritual quality, demonstrated between the dying person and their families. Many times staff demonstrated this affection towards the dying person and also their families at their most vulnerable and grief-stricken moments.

"We said the prayers with him. They'd be a consolation to him 'cos he liked the prayers, he liked the Mass. He went to Mass here; he had it in the room. He liked that."

"The three of us stayed with her. Little changes were occurring, the three of us were there. It was a great comfort to her that we were there."

"We were holding his hand all night….."

"All belonging to her were there…."

Spiritual aspects in this study, included the presence of family and friends at the bedside, touching and embracing by family and staff of the dying person, communication through conversation, laughter and story-telling and through listening to patients' worries and fears. Ongoing vigil and visits by family, friends and neighbours, all of which increased closer to the moment of death, provided a healing and comforting presence to the dying and strength to the family.

An Epiphany
During this study an unusual event occurred as I walked through the ward in the Palliative Care Unit late one Spring evening. As I passed the door of one of the families included in the study, I noticed Mr G sitting at the bedside of his dying wife. He called me in. I sat at the bedside unsure of what I could say, as his wife struggled to breath with an oxygen mask. Mrs G was too weak to speak. As the minutes went by Mrs G started to finger a little prayer book resting on the bedclothes. I opened it for her. Suddenly her husband gestured

towards the little book and said "She wants you to read some prayers to her." At first I didn't know how to react as I had never read prayers to a patient before and since I was the researcher, I thought, maybe this was Pastoral Care's role. But I opened the little book and as I read several prayers, Mrs G began to relax. Mr G thanked me and after a few words I left. A few days later as I passed the door, Mr G beckoned me in to the room again and asked "Would you read a few more prayers with my wife, she liked it so much the last time." Once more I read the same prayers and Mrs G whispered the words with us both. Mrs G died two days later. I phoned Mr G one week after his wife's death to enquire how Mrs G died and whether he would like to come in and talk. He said he would like to. I explained about the interview and the tape-recorder. He said that was fine. Mr G was a very gentle man, a sheep-farmer who lived ten miles away. He said, "My wife was the best wife a man could ever have and I am heart broken. It is now springtime and she would have loved the lambs." During the interview he cried and remained silent for intervals. As Mr G left, he turned and said"She loved when you said the prayers with her. She said that was special and you were special……. "I learnt from this epiphany, that no matter what our feelings are of awkwardness or embarrassment, as professionals - we need to step outside our expected roles and fulfil the small requests of our patients and meet them and their families on another level. These are barriers that need to be crossed. These are the loving gestures that will be long remembered by patients and their families.

An important link between illness and religious and spiritual needs was shown in a study by Koenig (1998). Among 330 consecutively admitted medical patients over 60 years of age, 85% used religion to help them cope to at least a moderate extent and 40% cited religion as the single most important factor in their coping. A high prevalence of religious coping has been shown to be present in people with end-stage kidney disease (Tix & Frasier, 1998), AIDS (Kaldjian, 1998), heart disease (Saudia, 1991) and cancer (Ginsburg, 1995; Roberts, 1997; Halstead & Fernsler, 1994). In my study on the moment of death, although the sample size of 20 patients and their families is smaller in number than Koenig (1998), I found that of 20 families interviewed by me, 95% (19 families) stated that their religion helped them cope. What emerges from the above study and also from my findings in this study on the moment of death is the duty imposed on us as professionals to be aware of and enter into dialogue with our patients and their relatives in the area of spirituality and its relevance to them.

Soul Pain

Serious illness regularly triggers questions of a spiritual nature, questions of meaning, value and relationships. These can be defined in the domain known as "spiritual pain". This is expressed by dying patients asking "Is God punishing me?" "What is the meaning of my life?" "What happens to me after I die?" Kearney (1996) describes soul pain, as:

"....... a particular type of suffering which is experienced by those close to death. For many the word soul may have religious connotations and can be understood as some vague and ethereal phantasm that is somehow in opposition to the physical and earthly part of ourselves and more likely to be at home in the "next world" than in this.

Soul can be described in the more classical sense as referring to the "psyche". The psyche is at the very heart of human experience. To describe someone as "soulful" is not to describe them as having transcended their humanity, but as one who is filled with the flesh and feeling of the world." An example of this type of "soul pain" expressed in this study is in an elderly farmer's description of his wife's fear and anxiety as death approaches, before dying a peaceful death two days later:

"In the room at night she started crying "Where am I going.... what am I to believe......" That affected her something awful. "Am I going into a big dark hole or is there a hereafter or am I going to meet my maker....?"

Soul pain is the experience of an individual who has become disconnected and alienated from the deepest and most fundamental aspect of themselves. Soul pain will often manifest physically as symptoms that do not respond to usually successful forms of treatment. Fig 5.1 demonstrates "the Iceberg Phenomenon" (Kearney, 1996), showing how soul pain representing trapped deep emotion can often be expressed by patients as unresolved physical pain. If these deep emotions are unrecognized, perhaps their only way out is through physical pain. Image-work may allow buried emotion express itself and so reduce physical and soul pain (Kearney, 1996).

Fig 5.1

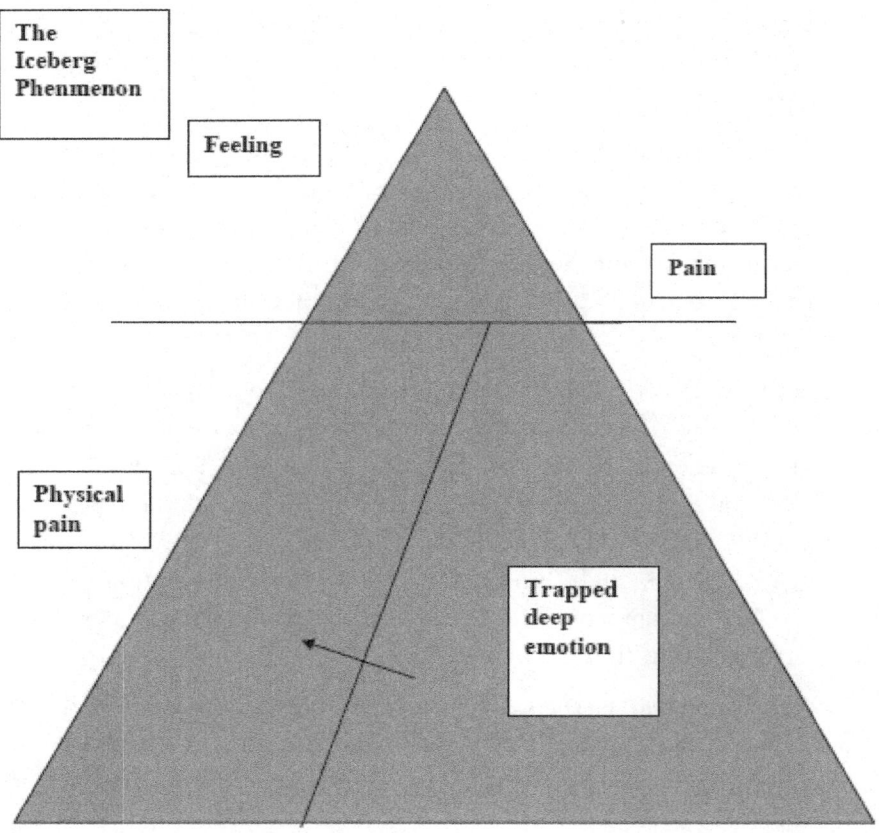

Thus palliative medicine physicians and general physicians find themselves in situations that require skill and sensitivity in assessing the spiritual needs of their patients (Marr & Billings, 2007; Puchalski, 2002). Physicians must be aware that they are not alone in caring for dying patients. They must remember that they are part of a multidisciplinary team including nurses, social workers and chaplains (Steinhauser & Clipp, 2000). A physician may initiate questions of a spiritual nature with a patient such as "what part does faith and spirituality play in your life?"

This demonstrates to the patient that the physician is aware of that aspect of their life. Physicians can then simply suggest whether the patient would like to talk further with a chaplain. Although physicians may not be responsible for solving the psycho-social or spiritual needs of the patient, acknowledging the presence and complexity of these needs is a way of actively affirming the patient as a whole person (Steinhauser & Clipp, 2000). We still have systems of care that do not encorporate spirituality in the care of patients.

Education
However, medical professionals are recognizing those inadequacies in the care of the dying and the interest in spirituality in medicine is growing (Puchalski 1998). There is a growing interest in spiritual education in medical schools and residency training that began around 1990 in the U. S. (Marr & Billings 2007). By 1999, almost 50% of 126 medical schools in the U.S. have taught courses on spirituality and medicine (Koenig, 1999).

In a survey of empirical studies published in leading Palliative Care journals between 1994 and 1998, 6.3% of studies included spiritual or religious variables in these journals, compared to 1 % reported in a similar study of the Journal of the American Medical Association, The Lancet, and The New England Journal of Medicine (Chochinov 2005). Marr & Billings (2007), provide us with the domains that can be used in Spirituality Education:

1. Communication of bad news

2. Concepts of suffering and spiritual distress

3. Data of links between spirituality/religion and health outcomes

4. Differences between spirituality and religion

5. How spiritual and cultural factors influence the doctor/ patient relationship

6. Taking a spiritual history

7. Addressing spiritual needs

8. Spiritual considerations in bereavement care

Training in spirituality involves developing fundamental knowledge skills and attitudes about the realm of human existence and clinical practice and touches on issues of professional role boundaries, personal competency and self confidence in intense interpersonal encounters and crosscultural care surrounding care of the dying (Marr & Billings, 2007). According to Millar & Chibnall (2005), medical care that recognizes and supports the spiritual nature of human beings, promotes spiritual well-being that many patients are seeking at the end of life. Clearly patients with serious medical conditions frequently suffer psycho-socio-spiritual pain that is inadequately addressed by modern health care. Additional research to improve the effectiveness of intervention to meet their needs is important and necessary. Already Irish doctors are being trained to help cancer patients with spiritual pain as demonstrated by conferences organised by the Irish cancer Society and the Irish Psycho-Oncology Group, Cork, June 6th 2008, with keynote speakers such as Prof Richard Groves, Palliative Care Specialist, Oregon, United States (IMN, 2008). Palliative medicine provides holistic care to all patients and this holistic care must involve taking care of the physical, psychological, social and spiritual needs of the patient. Already many hospices in Ireland incorporate the religious and spiritual preferences of patients and their relatives and since Ireland has become a multicultural society the integration of diverse religious beliefs in palliative care is becoming more apparent.

Attitudes to Spirituality and Ritual in this study on the Moment of Death.

19 out of the 20 families interviewed expressed an interest in their faith. 1 family stated they had no beliefs in an organised religion but believed in the after-life. See Table 6.1. (Chapter 6). The families who expressed an interest in their faith showed appreciation for the rituals and prayers offered by nurses and doctors and Pastoral Care at the bedside. 17 families were of the Catholic faith. They described the prayers and rituals of the priests blessing as a source of comfort and relief to them in their grief. All of these families placed rosary beads and the crucifix in the hands of the dying. These families also expressed how they felt the dying person would appreciate their prayers as they had appreciated prayer throughout their life. The families felt that the dying person could still hear their comforting conversations and prayers at the bedside while they were dying. The 2 families of the Church of Ireland faith appreciated the pastor praying over them and the dying person, while holding each others hands. They felt stronger through this and felt it was a beautiful gesture. The family who expressed no beliefs in an organised religion still believed there was an afterlife and that their father was going to a better place. They spoke of his spirit visiting the places he knew well in his lifetime before his death and a warmth present in the room after their father died. At the same time they expressed a lot of anger towards staff before and after their father's death. The absence of a strong religious belief did not take from this families' sense of the spiritual and the afterlife. I noted this as I proceeded with the study and learned from this to differentiate between religion and spirituality, where one person can follow a religious code and another may not but still have a sense of the spiritual.

Chapter 6:
Death and Dying in Ireland:
Conclusions and Some Future Research Approaches

Review

The purpose of this study is to enquire qualitatively into relatives' experience of the moment of death in a Specialist Palliative Care Unit (SPCU). A purposeful sampling strategy was used to identify families of dying patients in a city hospice in the Mid-West of Ireland. This study is unique in attempting to examine the moment of death in a SPCU and in maximizing recall by interviewing relatives early in their bereavement. To date the moment of death in a hospice setting has been largely unexplored.

Figure 6.1 demonstrates a Venn diagram outlining the interconnection between three key areas involved in this study: Qualitative Research, Irish cultural traditions of death and dying and Holistic care of the dying person and their families, physically, emotionally, spiritually and psychologically as a community, and in the Specialist Palliative Care Unit. All areas are interwoven and implicitly connected with this study on the moment of death. At the centre of all three areas and central to the study itself are the dying person and their families.

Fig 6.1 Venn diagram demonstrating key areas of this study

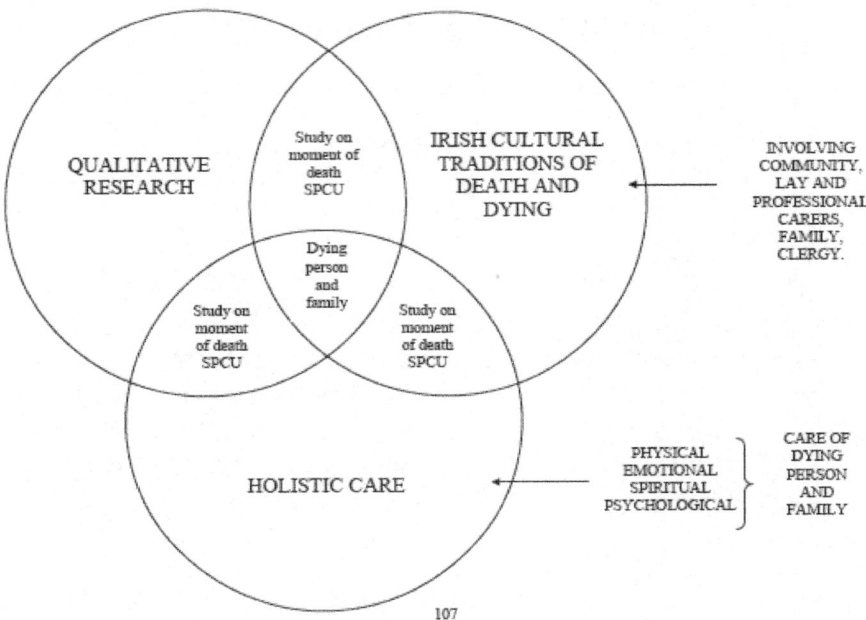

In this study, 29 adults including 3 teenagers from 20 families were interviewed on average 22 days (range 8-42 days) after the death of a close family member in a SPCU. There was a rich and detailed response to the invitation to describe the moment of death. Additional major themes were: vigil and the importance of being present; qualities of the staff; value of ritual and prayer; the open environment of the SPCU.

Palliative Care is a public health issue because everyone will die. This study describes dying and death. We cannot hear the stories of the dead. We can try to hear the stories of those who have witnessed dying. These relatives cared deeply for the individual who was dying. They observed every detail, attending to their role and observing the role of others. They are valuable witnesses.

As doctors working in Palliative Medicine we care for people who ultimately will die yet rarely are we present at the moment of their death. Much published work on the moment of death has been written by anthropologists and sociologists but not by those directly involved in the care of the dying (Glaser & Strauss 1968; Kastenbaum & Normand, 1990; Kellehear, 1984; Seale, 1995). In this moment of death study I seek to describe the needs and circumstances of dying people and their relatives, the ways in which these needs were met and to highlight areas in which improvements are needed for the future. The purpose of this study is to illustrate how a doctor as a researcher can learn posthumously from family witnesses what it is to experience the moment of death in a Specialist Palliative Care Unit (Donnelly, 2009 (a)).

Palliative Care programmes continue to demonstrate that enlightened and dedicated care can markedly reduce the suffering of patients with advanced cancer and their families; yet Kastenbaum (1999) questions why the vast experience acquired has not yet been translated into a vision of the moment of death. The moment of death has become increasingly marginalised. Valentine (2007) in interviews with 25 bereaved individuals suggests that the experience of the moment of death has been largely overlooked and that dying loved ones' final moments may be experienced as highly significant. The purpose of this moment of death study in a Specialist Palliative Care Unit was for a doctor as researcher to learn from witnesses of death of their relatives about the experience of their moment of death. The impact of death in our society is not appreciated and is easily underestimated. There is power and influence in a dignified death, which can have a profound effect on the family and those close to the person who has died (Ellershaw, 2003). This moment of death is a narrow door and according to Kastenbaum (1999), is of such significance to the dying patient, their relatives and carers, in its actuality and not simply as a concept, that it needs to be brought into the light and examined more closely (Weinrick & Curtis, 2003).

In Kastenbaum's (1999) view, the moment of death enquiry is useful in delineating core human values, fears and hopes - all of life being encapsulated in that moment, that brings both meaning and cessation. In my study on the moment of death in a specialist palliative care unit, I aim to capture this moment of death by my presence with family relatives of the dying patient and I also aim to empower health care workers for the future in their care of the dying by illuminating the sensitivities and needs of dying patients and their relatives at the moment of death. The moment of death has been a compelling image and dominant concept throughout much of history. Kastenbaum (1999) suggests that the term has become destabilised by technological advances. Hospice has said so little when cultural tradition says so much about the last moment of life. Although death is a rite of passage in which we will all participate, we understand little of what is valued at the end of life (Steinhauser, 2000) This study looks at the mystique of the moment of death in what Kastenbaum & Normand (1990) consider "a nearly vanished world". The authors also suggest that if we look closely at how we die, we will be challenged as to how we live. The actual moment of death had much traditional significance and has also functioned as an important symbolic reality for many years in many cultures but particularly in Ireland (Donnelly, 1999 (a)&(b); Kastenbaum, 1999; Aries, 1974. Lysaght, 1986, 1995, 1997; Tyers, 1992; Van Gennep, 1961) This moment of death analysis, follows a study on traditions of death and dying in Ireland and Scotland (Donnelly, 1999(a)&(b)) From that folklore collection it was clear that the moment of death was highly significant for the carer, family and their communities. The moment of death was sacred. The next question is whether this moment still has significance. If so, should not the doctors who claim to serve the people at the time of their dying, enquire about this experience?

In this study we aim to define the needs and concerns of dying patients and their families in a Specialist Palliative Care Unit, by directly illuminating the interactions and dialogue between the dying patient, their families and carers in the days leading up to the moment of death and the moment itself by means of interviews with bereaved relatives 1-6 weeks after the death. This study is confined exclusively to families and patients dying in the Specialist Palliative Care Unit and comparisons are not made with those dying at home or in the acute hospital. Separate analysis of dying patients and their familes at home and in the acute hospital are the subject of other studies (Donnelly, 2006; Donnelly, 2009 (b)). Although qualitative analysis allows for the subjectivity of both researcher and participant, the purpose and aim as here in my research study is to discover the interviewees own framework of meanings, avoiding as much as possible imposing any preconceptions structures or assumptions that I may have. In so far as these matters such as the dying persons symptoms, management or medication arise incidentally as part of the experience of the relatives as recounted by them spontaneously to myself, they are then incorporated and analyzed by me in this study.

Similarly, while neither praise nor criticism nor their evaluation of our treatment of the deceased is sought by me from the relatives either directly or by inference or suggestion, should such emerge in their spontaneous conversation it will be included in my final analysis.

Method
This is a qualitative enquiry (Clark, 1997) into the phenomenon of the moment of death as experienced by relatives in a Specialist Palliative Care Unit (SPCU) in the Mid- West of Ireland. Those eligible to the study were relatives of patients who died within the Palliative Care Unit. The Pastoral Care team helped to identify patients who fulfilled the inclusion criteria. Using a purposeful (Mays & Pope, 1995 (b)) sampling strategy, 27 families were identified. Purposeful sampling is the selection of information rich cases for study in depth (Patton, 1990) with a view to understanding something about these cases without needing to generalise to all such cases. Clark (1997) states that within the approach of purposive sampling, it is considered acceptable to limit the number of subjects in a study to the point where saturation of new information has been achieved. It is not considered necessary to continue gathering data long after it has become clear that nothing new is being learned. This was so in this study on the moment of death where patients and families were recruited until no new information was being gathered. I included those patients likely to die in the SPCU, those likely to die within 1week and 6 months of first contact and those likely to have at least one family member present at the time of death. All patients and their families had been informed of their diagnosis and prognosis many

months before my first introduction. Exclusion criteria were, those that had no available visiting companion, where death was not imminent within 6 months, where family or friends refused to be included in the study or where family member or companion had not been present at the death. The recruitment of patients and their families originated from both city and surrounding rural areas. As only 1 family was from a rural background (19 families were from the city) urban/ rural comparison was not possible. The setting of this study in a Specialist Palliative Care Unit was open to recruitment of adult participants both male and female, from diverse backgrounds, occupations, race and religion. Children were excluded from the study, as my supervisor and I considered it inappropriate to impose on them and their families at this time.

As a researcher and medical doctor who had no clinical commitment to the patient, I adopted a researcher role solely – i.e. visiting the patient and their family on a daily basis. On initial visits to the patient and their families I explained the purpose of my study and asked would they wish to participate. I did not wear a white coat. Initially I introduced myself as a doctor doing research, however the response from both patient and relative was neutral, sometimes I was met with a blank stare. After this experience had occurred several times I decided that "research" was not the right word to use so I said that "myself and my supervisor were doing a study hoping to improve the care for the dying and their relatives". The reaction was much more positive and a there was a greater understanding of what was involved.

I adopted Kellehear's (1989) ethical approach to research by emphasising empathy and interpersonal sensitivity as critical for this study. At such a sensitive time in the families bereavement, the empathy and consideration required to obtain family consent for interviews necessitated considerable time and effort (Rinck, 1997; Ross & Cornbleet, 2003).

Due to the families' prior acceptance of the presence of professional carers in the care of their dying relative in the hospice setting, they were very open and willing to dialogue with and trust in the researcher. There is no doubt that this fact assisted in the building of a close and open relationship between myself as a doctor and researcher and the families throughout the study, continuously enriching the data. On the first day of meeting relatives at the beginning of the study, at the bedside of the patient I offered a written explanation to the relative of what the study involved. I also explained to the patient what the study involved. After the death of the patient I obtained verbal consent by phone from the relative to do the interview and obtained written consent from them on the day of the interview. Having spoken with the relatives on many occasions over several months prior to the interview, I contacted family members by phone 8-42 days after death, who had been present at the moment of death of their relative. A total of 20 families agreed to be interviewed and were finally included in the study from the 27 initially recruited. 5 patients died before I could sufficiently familiarise myself with relatives, 1 family agreed to be included in the study but declined to be interviewed after their relative died and 1 patient died while temporarily outside the Palliative Care Unit. See Table 6.1 showing statistics of interviews. See Appendix 8.5 on demographics of patients in study. In accordance with Kastenbaum (1999) when he states, that no palliative care program should compromise the welfare of its patients by intrusive research procedures, I adhered to strict ethical guidelines.

Table 6.1

Details of families interviewed

No. of families recruited	27
Patients dying outside SPCU	1
Patients discharged home	1
Patients dying within 1 week of recruitment	4
Families declining interview	1
No. of families interviewed	20

No. of Adults interviewed	26
No. of teenagers interviewed	3
No. of males interviewed	10
No. of females interviewed	19
Individual interviews	13
Group interviews of 2 people	6
Group interviews of 4 people	1
Average duration (mins) of Interviews	43
Range (mins)	20-70
Families of Catholic faith	17
Families of Church of Ireland	2
Families of no religion	1
SPCU as place of interview	16
Home as place of interview	4

I obtained ethical approval from the Mid- West Ethics and Research Committee. See Appendix 8.1. Addington-Hall (2001) reminds us that after death interviews with bereaved respondents are an important tool in the repertoire of researchers, evaluating the quality of end of life care. Not only this, but the period between the experience and the recollection is crucial to the accuracy of the recalled information and the ease to which it is recalled (Bradley 1990). Addington-Hall (2001) states that the retrospective or after death approach to measuring the quality of care in the last months of life is well established in the UK and is an important source of information on the last months of life. Similar methods have been used in other studies by Lynn & Teno (1997), during which bereaved relatives provided information on patients' last three days of life. One of the criticisms made of after-death surveys is that bereaved people are likely to be experiencing extreme emotions and are therefore unreliable as sources of information on events before death. Addington-Hall (2001) also reminds us that negative comments about services may be dismissed as being a consequence of relatives' bereavement related anger and not to be taken seriously. However, in understanding these comments I disagree with the dismissing of relatives emotions and statements as being inconsequential. In my qualitative enquiry I interviewed families 1-7 weeks after death of their relative, their emotions and sentiments expressed to me were true and valid for each individual through whose eyes we are given a vision of the moment of death. Without their stories though given with emotion, we would not have a unique and privileged encounter with the persons hour of death.

The short interval in my study of 1 week, on average 22 days, with a range of 8-42 days, between the death of the patient and interview with relatives, allowed for maximum recall of information by the families on the death of their relative. This time factor compares with that of previous studies of intervals of 1week- 2years in bereavement studies (Cartwright & Seale 1990; Higgonson, Priest & McCarthy, 1994; Hinton, 1996; Ahmedazai & Morton, 1998; Stroebe & Schut, 2003).

According to Addington –Hall (2001) memory and recall are affected by grief, where memory may be selectively biased as a function of the frequency and saliency of an event. Less salient events tend to be underreported whereas salient events tend to be over reported. Also, highly emotional events are recalled better than neutral ones. The period between the experience and the recollection is crucial to the accuracy of the recalled information and the ease to which it is recalled. There is strong evidence to suggest that the shorter the intervening period the easier it is to recall information (Addington-Hall, 2001). However in after-death surveys this needs to be balanced against ethical concerns about distressing bereaved people so soon after death. Qualitative research with in-depth interviews can be safely and ethically conducted with bereaved families, if performed sensitively according to Hynson & Aroni (2006). The authors' study examined the impact of qualitative interview research process on bereaved parents and which elements enhance the experience of research participation. They found that although the majority of parents chose to participate in the in-depth interviews for altruistic reasons, many described the research process through interview as personally beneficial.

Personal contact with interviewees is the most satisfying and engaging stage of enquiry and continually offers new insights into the lived world of the people, making the research an exciting and enriching experience (Steiner, 1996). In the moment of death study all my interviews are tape-recorded, in order to have record of the nuances of meaning and subtleties of expression in the different families. Each interview recording took three to seven hours to transcribe in detail. The average duration of the interviews was 43 minutes with a range of between 20-70 minutes. See Table 6.1.

The interview itself was part of a continuum of observation and analysis from the very beginning of the study. From the initial contact with the family, I as researcher analyzed continually, through observation and dialogue and with the aid of note taking, the family and their interaction with their dying relative for many weeks and months in advance on the ward in the Palliative Care Unit. The family became familiar and closer to me and I to them for many weeks and months prior to the interview. Patients and their families became enthusiastic and altruistic at the idea of contributing their own stories to the study in order to improve the care for other patients and families in the future. As patients lay in their beds or sat out at the bedside, they recounted to me the stories of their struggles, hopes and fears on facing death and of the needs of their families. There was a sense of urgency in the telling of their stories and a need to be listened to.

Of utmost importance in this study is the necessity for the family to trust the researcher and I cannot over emphasize the value of this trust between the patient, their families and the researcher. Relatives are naturally protective of their dying relative and are particularly sensitive at this time, therefore, it is essential that a delicate balance of sensitivity and compassion are maintained by the researcher in order to nurture a trusting relationship. It is a dynamic process that slowly evolves and takes shape day by day due to regular consistent contact by the researcher with the family and patient for periods anything from a few minutes to several hours each day, listening to the difficulties and emotional upsets of the relatives and the patient and accompanying them for some time on their journey.

It is vital that the family see the researcher interact with the dying patient on a daily basis, for a relationship of trust to develop between researcher and patient and so between the family and the researcher. This is the essence of enriching, truthful, fulfilling and ethical research for both participants and researcher. In this way, I concur with Seymour (2001), who identified responses to the emotional needs of companions, sharing of information and knowledge and the expression of personal feelings as encouraging the development of trusting relationships in the Intensive Care Unit (ICU) setting.

I was aware of the need to be non-intrusive, non-contributory and of not bringing personal or preconceived notions to the interview. The open-ended questions allowed the relatives to speak freely and openly of their experiences. I exercised great care to avoid bias by direct personal or leading questioning. In this study on the moment of death, the interviews sometimes took the form of a conversation in an informal and interactive way allowing topics to be discussed as they arose. Even though the topic was highly emotional for the grieving relatives, I allowed them to talk for long periods without allowing my empathy to develop an emotional attachment or dependency. Meeting family members prior to the patient's death facilitated the early post-bereavement visit. Due to the families prior acceptance of the presence of professional carers in the care of their dying relative in the Specialist Palliative Care Unit, they were very open and willing to dialogue with and trust in me, as researcher. There is no doubt that this fact assisted in the building of a close and trusting relationship between myself as a doctor and researcher and the families throughout the study. This trusting relationship enriched the data considerably. This relationship of trust between me as researcher and the family member was evident in many ways, however two particular situations demonstrated this to me. On one particular day I had to meet an elderly farmer whose wife had died in the Palliative Care Unit in the previous two weeks. I had met him on many occasions over the previous few weeks with his dying wife. He arrived at the reception and introduced me to his daughter. I shook hands with them and greeted them both. I was about to guide him to my office to the right down a long corridor when he turned to me and said "I'd like to go to Mass in the chapel, will you come?" I said I would and all three of us went to Mass before the interview.

I had met with a young wife and mother many times on the ward as she sat with her dying husband. I remember contacting her by phone a week after her husband's death and how I said that if the interview was too much for her there was no need to worry and I enquired about how she was coping. She said it was very difficult but followed on by saying that she really wanted to come in for the interview and appreciated all the help that was given to her family and her husband in the Palliative Care Unit. It was this lady's insistence even in the midst of her grief to travel a distance for interview that made me realise the importance of the relationship of trust and familiarity over the previous several months. The interview included her three teenage children and she spoke openly, honestly and poignantly about her husband's death.

Although I had built a close relationship with the family for many weeks or months prior to and at the time of death of their relative, the interview and posthumous conversations always centred on the patient and their needs and as relating to their family at that particular juncture. Interviews took place in a relaxed and non-interrogative environment, emphasizing clarification of the experience and description and reaction to the moment of death by the relatives. Conversations were never of a personal nature. This concept is supported by Spradley (1979) where he states that the interviewer must avoid allowing the interview to turn into a therapeutic situation where dependency develops and possible emotional distress.

The interaction is neither anonymous and neutral as when a subject responds to a survey questionnaire, nor as personal and emotional as a therapeutic interview (Spradley, 1979).

At the same time it was important to guard against becoming impersonal and detached and this influenced my choice against using paper questionnaires as a form of data collection in this study. I felt that this method would be anonymous and devoid of personal contact and that personal contact was extremely important for the families and for me as researcher at this sensitive time, in order to witness emotions and expressions of the family at first hand allowing the research to be more "real" and enriching.

Interviewees were informed by me of the availability of bereavement support from the Social Work Team. I gave those interested in bereavement counselling the name and telephone number of the Senior social worker. I also informed the Senior social worker of the names of those who were interested in bereavement counselling. 4 families said they would avail of counseling at a later date. I informed the Senior Social Worker of any additional concerns arising from the interview process, which I as a doctor had observed.

Mindful of the sensitivity of the topic (Addington – Hall & McPhearson, 2001; Stroebe, Stroebe & Schut, 2003) emphasis was placed on minimising potential distress to the families and at all times being tactful and considerate. In the process of engagement with relatives of the dying person, I concur with McQueen (1997), who suggests that empathy and engagement are important in order to respond to cues and anticipate needs of relatives. Hunt (1991) has stated how informality and friendliness are increasingly used by professional carers, to overcome barriers. In this study, I introduced myself to families, one to six months prior to death of their relative and as I responded in an appropriate, caring and friendly way, an ongoing, trusting, informal relationship was nurtured and maintained with the patients and their families.

I obtained verbal consent from the family members on the phone prior to the interview and written consent on the day of the interview, giving a full explanation of the format and aims of the interview. I informed the families that they could withdraw from the interview at any time and that anonymity would be insured by changing their names. The venue and the time of interview were at the discretion of the interviewee. I also gave a full explanation that I would be recording and transcribing the interview, with the possibility that the contents of the interview would be used as an oral presentation or written publication for education purposes. Anonymity and confidentiality were again assured with the confirmation that the data given would be stored in a locked drawer in my office to which I only held the key. I assured family members that they could withdraw at any time from the study, after which data arising from their participation would be destroyed.

In this study, there were factors that affected the time interval between death and the interviews taking place. Twenty families were interviewed. All were contacted by phone one week after the death of their relative. 13 of those families agreed to be interviewed at 1-3 weeks after the death. 7 of those families requested time to grieve, and were not ready for interview until between 3-6 weeks after the death of their relative.

Several families stated directly after the interview that they found the interview of help to them in their grief. A mother whose husband died, attended for interview with her daughter. Both stated that they found attending the interview a consolation and that they had both wished to attend to show their appreciation for the care given to their relative in the Palliative Care Unit. Another lady whose uncle had died three weeks previously in the Palliative Care Unit, had lost her brother also in the intervening few weeks and wished to come to the interview to share her grief. I had developed a trusting relationship with this lady while visiting her dying uncle on the ward.

I attended one of the patient's deaths in a researcher capacity. I was invited to do so by the family. Many of the other deaths of patients involved in the study were during the night. On other occasions my supervisor and I agreed that it would be too intrusive to attend at such a private moment. At no stage of my interview with the 20 families in the study did relatives mention that they or the dying person express a wish to staff or otherwise at any stage to hasten the dying process. Two families overall expressed anger at initial stages of the interview, however the 20 families interviewed expressed ease, comfort and satisfaction with care and treatment of their relative. I noted the appreciation the patients and their families showed for a full detailed explanation of the aims of the study in the initial stages and also in the use of consent forms prior to the interview with relatives. Patients and their families became enthusiastic at the idea of contributing their own stories to the study as they explained that they wanted to help to improve the care of patients and their families in the future. As patients lay in their beds or sat out at the bedside, they told me the stories of their struggles, hopes and fears of facing death and of the needs of their families. There was a sense of urgency in the telling of their stories and a need to be listened to. These stories are incorporated in the findings of this study.

There was also a difference between interviews in the home setting and that of the Palliative Care Unit. Initially, as explained above, I asked the family by phone on first contact after the death of their relative, where they wished to have the interview. 4 out of 20 families expressed a wish for the interview at home (either due to difficulty getting into Palliative Care Unit or finding it difficult emotionally and psychologically to return to the place where their relative had died 16 families travelled to the Palliative Care Unit). See Table 6.1. As researcher, I discovered that when the interview was in my office in the Palliative Care Unit, I was in control of the process. When relatives were anxious, it was my duty to put them at ease. In the family home setting our roles were reversed. I was their guest and they were in control. Their duty was to put me at my ease and welcome me into their home. I was privileged to be there and beholden to them. Even though families seemed more at ease in their own homes, I did not notice any difference in the spontaneity of conversation or richness of the data obtained in both places.

These semi-structured interviews were tape-recorded on an average 22 days (range 8-42 days) after the death of the patient (Plant, 1996). Questions focused on the experience, description, emotions and needs of the dying patient and their relatives at the moment of death. See Appendix 8.4.

I used follow-up probes for more detailed information. I allowed the interviewee to speak freely without interruption. The authors Hynson & Aroni (2006) have found that the in the use of in-depth qualitative interviewing allowing the interviewee to determine the pace and content of the interview gave them a sense of empowerment and of being in control.

I recorded field-notes following each interview, to assist with interviewer debriefing and discussion with my supervisor. By maintaining a reflective diary, field notes and regular discussions with my supervisor, my professional and personal experiences were bracketed. The following is an extract from my field-notes recording a visit of a relative for interview in my office in the SPCU one week after his father's death.

"T's daughter S was due to have met me for the interview but as I waited at reception a young man in his early 30's appeared. He walked up to me and introduced himself as N, T's son. He was friendly and easygoing. I explained the reasons for the interview and he graciously nodded his head in agreement. We walked the long corridor to my office and still we talked.

I had been unable to find the Marantz tape-recorder so I was thinking of using another hoping in the back of my mind that it would work. N signed the consent form and we started the interview. N talked a lot about his father. He seemed to want to explain the reasons for his thoughts and feelings even to the minutest detail. He had stopped work two years previously so he could look after his father and never regretted it. In contrast to some difficult interviews I found N easy to listen to. (I notice that there is no doubt that one can react favourably to an interviewee and less so when the interview doesn't go as smoothly.) After the interview N said he would like to walk up to the ward where his father had died.

I accompanied N and on our way N stopped to chat with two nurses and a doctor who had looked after his father. I felt that it was a therapeutic visit for N and as we parted he said he was glad he had come to talk and to visit the room again where his father had died.

Before T left he told me a story about his four year old niece who had tried to cheer him up after his father's death. She said "N, Granda is now up in heaven cycling on his bike." N said his father had loved cycling.

I noted a calmness and acceptance in N. He had done all he could for his father and had done the right thing. There was a sense of completion and absence of any guilt. There was a natural sadness but also a sense of peace. I noted that this was not often the case comparing with the death of QP where it seemed a lack of forgiveness or unresolved issues left a sense of guilt and unease among the family. Being aware of this I have to guard against bias on my part by not reacting to the relatives anger or grief. "

The Pastoral Care team did not participate in the interviews. The sole role of the Pastoral Care team was to help me to identify the 20 consecutive patients and families who might fulfil the inclusion criteria. I met with a member of the Pastoral Care Team each morning. The member of the team I met included two members of the Sisters of the Little Company of Mary. We reviewed who had been admitted the day before and the night before, and who was due to be admitted that day. Of those patients, we identified those who would be most appropriate or suitable to the criteria outlined for inclusion in the study – i.e. Those patients with visiting relatives, those relatives who were considered more "open" and approachable or available for consent. Those patients who would be likely die in less than 6 months. Once patients were identified I introduced myself to the patients and their relatives visiting them each morning until the patients death.

Data collection and analysis occurred concurrently. Data was sourced through in-patient chart notes, observation notes, field notes and interviews. I transcribed the interviews verbatim beginning immediately after the interview. As discussed in Chapter 2, I adopted the constant comparative method as my method of data analysis. See Figure 2.5 & 2.6 (a) & (b) (Chapter 2), where the figures demonstrate the use of the constant comparative method in producing themes as demonstrated later in this chapter in my findings of this study.

The constant comparative method analyzes the qualitative data whereby the information gathered is coded into emergent themes or codes. All information gathered during the study are read and re-read. All transcripts are given a code number and identifying information removed in order to keep the data anonymous (Williams & Payne, 2003) article on depression in palliative care patients). The quality of data analysis depends on repeated, systematic searching of the data (Hammersley,1981). In an attempt to achieve this, as in the moment of death study, repeated coding was performed to review interpretations, in light of the new data gathered and as the new codes were generated, until no new insights were being gleaned (Riley, 1990). The interviews were initially read and coded independently by myself and my supervisor, using in vivo and conceptually derived codes (Densen & Lincoln, 1994; Green, 1998; Strauss & Corbin, 1998). Coding involved using actions or fragments of interview text to refine their fit to underlying concepts. The process was repeated until myself and my supervisor were satisfied that all the data could be interpreted in organized concepts (Lucas 2007). My supervisor and I worked together, agreeing on codes, concepts and emerging themes. In this combined process, systematically reviewing each interview, concepts gained further supporting evidence or were reduced in weighting, with outlying and possible deviance in analysis agreed upon. Thematic categories were then derived which encompassed similar codes. The constant comparative method allows the precise nature of each individual's view to be captured and recalled, as in this study on the moment of death, and data can be presented in a logical sequence in relation to the research questions addressed in the study (Hewitt-Taylor, 2001).

All analysis decisions were made by consensus. To validate findings and account for potential bias, a selection of transcripts were reviewed by an external qualitative researcher, David Clark, Professor of Medical Sociology (Visiting Professor of Hospice Studies to Trinity College Dublin and University College Dublin) and a Specialist in Qualitative Research, Lancaster University, U.K. Data saturation was achieved after the analysis of 20 interviews over a period of 6 months and recruitment ceased.

Findings

Of 27 families recruited, 20 families involving 26 adults and 3 teenagers agreed to be interviewed within 1-6 weeks (average 22 days) of the death of their relative. There were 13 individual interviews, one group of 4 people and six groups of 2 people each. The 10 men interviewed included husbands, sons, a nephew and a father. The 19 women interviewed included wives, daughters, sisters, a niece and a mother. 16 interviews took place in the Specialist Palliative Care Unit while 4 took place at home. See Table 6.1.

Recruitment and interviews of the 20 families occurred over 6 months. All families recruited for the study were white and all were Irish citizens. Thus the study was open to a broad crosssection of society. All families who agreed verbally to participate, when approached before the death of their relative, followed through with written consent for interviews after the death of their relative. This may reflect the value and efforts made by me, as researcher, in establishing a relationship of trust with the families in the SPCU, for many weeks and months, during their vigil. The themes that have emerged from data analysis in this study are detailed below. The themes have emerged in the context in which the death has occurred, that is the setting of the Specialist Palliative Care Unit.

The Moment of Death

There was a rich and detailed response to the invitation to describe the moment of death. In the interviews the moment of death was described as:

"very, very peaceful, just lovely, so calm, beautiful, a very happy death". One son described his mother's last moments as follows:" Most of us were all around, her six children and Daddy and her sister Aunty Kathleen. I says "mother, I love you" and she says "I love you too." Now she went to put her arm around my neck to say something to me.......... my mother had a beautiful, peaceful death."

A wife says her last few words to her dying husband, "I just bent over him and said "Are you happy Joe?" and he just smiled and that was the last."

The family observes closely, understanding that although their relative was unconscious "we all knew she was with us. She wasn't able to open her eyes but she was able to flick her eyes, you could see it."" They say the hearing is the last to go."" You could see in the eyebrows, he heard us". So they continued talking naturally, holding his hand and praying out loud.:" We were each side of the bed holding his hand……. we prayed for him…….. [we heard] the rattle in the throat and we knew then straight away that he was dying. Sr Anne brought in the candle then and she put the Mass on the television and she gave him the blessing…….. he gave a few little gasps and just died. His hand was under his chin just the same as a baby."

The descriptions are detailed, rich, poignant and honest "I went over and put my arms around her and I called Martha, Martha and she opened her eyes and gave a big smile and she was gone. Her lips quivered for a couple of seconds afterwards and then she was gone."

A young woman describes her sister's death:

"Mom said twenty minutes before she died, she was rubbing Katie's hand and she said "Katie, I love you and all your friends love you" and a tear rolled down from her eye and then twenty minutes later…… she was ready to go."

They had an understanding of the unconscious state "he was between two worlds. He wasn't fully in another world either." This is reminiscent of traditional Irish appreciation of a spirit world being close at hand at death. They understood that he visited "all the places that he loved" as he was dying, that "he did the rounds when he was in the coma." This family understood dying as an energetic event to which they reacted similarly "his whole body shook the moment he died like an energy surge going through it, like he jumped off a bridge" As he was dying, they checked his heart by putting their head on his chest, shouting at him to come back and then roared "we love you"….. and we know that was the last thing he heard". They understood that dead family members were "waiting for him…" and "his family had whipped him off."

Parents experienced their adult son's death in a quieter way. With a doctor, two nurses, the chaplain, two cousins, an aunt and a best friend present, she whispered to her 40 year old son "Mammy is here, Daddy is here" and all of a sudden he took three soft breaths and you'd think he was going to sleep."

For a wife who had not seen anybody die before "his opened eyes rolling", was very frightening… while for his daughter "I've seen people die before. He bowed out. It was very peaceful." For a Church of Ireland family "the hospice chaplain put his hand on Dad's head and he held my hand. I held my daughters. We said our prayers. It was absolutely beautiful experience for my daughter and me. It was my first time to be with somebody who passed on."

At night, the nurses brought a candle as a son continued to hold his dying fathers hand and talk to him. As the two night nurses prayed over his father, he felt very comfortable with his father dying, "it was just like a puff of air, there one second, gone the next."

One family believed that H's own serenity determined how gently he died. "He only gave two gasps and he was gone. Kindly enough both of us heard it the gentle rattle, the lovely gentle rattle ……his serenity…. he gave only two gasps and he was gone.. He was lovely to be with, a beautiful expression on his face….. a beautiful smile. He just went out like the candle that was flickering. Oh, he didn't rebuke, he didn't, he was so gentle…. like a baby. 'Twas his gentle nature. He was lovely to be with, a lovely aura."

Poignant metaphors describe the scene visually "Sr N descended upon him to tell him that he was going home, but in a lovely spiritual way. We ran in like a flock of birds, like a flock of gulls, kissing and hugging him. It was so beautiful." This family describe how Frank gave them hope as he was dying "He'd never upset us. You'd come into [see] him and he'd say he was fine and he may not have been…… he'd give you hope."

The nurses "just stood quietly by." The staff did not intervene when a daughter shouted painfully "speak to me, speak to me" They left her to "howl" until she eventually realised that he wasn't going to speak. "They left her which was rather nice."

There was a "stunned silence" at the moment of her fathers death even though the death was long expected "it happened very, very quickly at the end" No words were spoken until they left the room eventually and were given tea by the staff.

There is an art in being able to just stand quietly by. Another family appreciated being left: "the staff then disappeared" and appreciated all being together. "We all shared sitting beside him, holding his hand. We all said so many lovely things to him- to tell him we all loved him and we were going to miss him terribly." They name each family member who was present usually between six and fourteen in number, summing up with pride and satisfaction "all belonging to her were there."

Some family members regretted missing the actual moment of death of their aunt "I'd love to have been there" but took consolation in the fact that her son was there "she loved him and he loved her. He held her hand the whole day." A son describes how it was so important to be there for his fathers last breath "we were there for the last couple of minutes."

There is an art born of skill and experience in being able to create an atmosphere that "was easier than being at home". A son describes "the family talked away as naturally as if they were visiting at home," at the bedside of his dying mother.

The impending moment of death was heralded by Pastoral Care saying prayers with the family, by bringing in candles and later signifying that death was even closer by the nurse lighting the candle and occasionally putting it into the patient's hand. Catholic families spontaneously or guided by pastoral care recited the litany of prayers (rosary) and specific prayers for the dying. "I never saw such prayers. I prayed for 24 hours-absolutely unreal. We all took turns and the nuns were brilliant."

As previously noted, (Donnelly, 2006; Steinhauser, 2000), the dying patient needs to reciprocate or there is the need for generativity, service, selflessness by the carers and the dying patient. (Ref Home MOD) there is mutual caring bond between the dying person and the attending relative. As NT is dying she asked her husband "Are you happy now, John? I'm handing you over into God's hands." He replied "I am" and he felt a strange sensation coming over him that gave him strength for that moment and the rest of the evening. NT died that evening.

Families perceived that their mother" did not labour one bit" even though her eyes were wide open and she was gasping, "I thought it was lovely, honest to God. I was glad I was there." Others compare the posture of their relative "like a baby, his hand was under his chin, just the same as a baby." They were knowledgeable and vigilant for signs that "he had taken the change" "the rattle in the throat. We knew straight away he was dying."

In all of the interviews, the moment of death is marked by presence - individually, silently and in community - and the attention of family and staff totally on one person including prayer - ritualized in words and candles. It is a moment to be witnessed. This is part of the tradition and an expression of love. The palliative care staff understand this completely. As described in this study - presence, vigil and dignity are highly valued by families. Our study reiterates Toscani's (2005) study of forty Italian hospitals, where time spent with family and close friends, being kept clean and not dying alone mattered most." Then we got all together [by the bedside], then the Ryans and Doyles were all chatting away. We all talked away as naturally as if you were visitin'…….. it was more homely than being at home."

"There was all her nieces there, I was there, her two daughters, her son, her nephews, her two son-in-laws. All belonging to her were there."

"They never left him on his own for a minute."

"The nurses were in changed her nightdress, combed her hair and fixed her up. It was all done with dignity."

Awareness of life beyond death

A consistent theme in this study is the awareness of life beyond death. The conviction that individual human beings survive death, perhaps eternally, has persisted and frequently dominated throughout Western civilization (Momeyer 1995). Awareness of life after death was prevalent in the Irish people in the past where they had a pervading sense of the spiritual world in their daily life (Donnelly 1999 (a)). This possibility of life after death permeates our study. I asked family relatives at the interviews, what they thought happened to a person after they die. See Appendix 8.4. The reason for this rare intrusion into objectivity was to analyze its influence, if any, on the families' attitude to the death and dying of their relative. One family who said that they had no religious beliefs nevertheless described the presence of another world for their dying father:

"He was between two worlds. He wasn't fully in the other world yet."

A man whose mother had died describes his own beliefs:

"To me when I die I'm goin' home……"

A niece describes her uncle who had died the previous week:

"I felt that night that he died, that he was going to a better place. He'll look down on us and keep an eye on us because he was a good man…."

A nephew describes how his dying aunt would look up and say to him each day during the week before her death:

"Heaven is a beautiful place; no one should be frightened."

An elderly farmer tells us of his wife's fear and anxiety, questioning the existence of life after death, before dying a peaceful death two days later:

"In the room at night she started crying "Where am I going…. what am I to believe……" That affected her something awful….

"Am I going into a big dark hole or is there a hereafter or am I going to meet my maker? "

A husband speaks of his wife's religious faith after her death:

"...Definitely gone to heaven, definitely gone to heaven. She was a great Catholic, absolutely brilliant. She was a great person to teach the faith to the children. You know when you'd say the rosary a smile would come on her face. Wonderful person..... she's only gone for a while until we meet again."

Vigil.
Being present as a person is dying is an important Irish tradition. People were laughing and crying, and going back over family stories "he would have loved it himself". Families emphasise that they were there to the very end and that the whole family was there "there were about 10 in the room" For one man being present all the time was important because "he actually remembered the day his sister was born and he wasn't going to leave her the day she died" The mobile phone broadens the possibility of vigil as a daughter travelling from London prayed with her dying mother on the mobile phone. It was important to be there "he was never left alone"; equally it was important that the patient "knew we were there" They understand the value of "actually seeing a person going into death" even though "it was a fright" because previously "I didn't see my father die." as a result "I always felt he wasn't dead."

A husband describes his son's presence at his wife's death. "My son John was there. He treated her as home. She loved him and he loved her. He held her hand the whole day, that day."

Families are also curious about prognosis, watching for signs from the patient of "fading away in the bed". Some understand how difficult it is to know but others struggle to find out "Lara literally wanted a day, an hour...I said she's going to ask (the doctor) for seconds now!"

As described in the findings of my study, presence, vigil and dignity are highly valued by the dying patient and their families. Toscani (2005) demonstrates in a study of forty different Italian hospitals, that the most important and basic attributes of how patients die, are the time spent with family and close friends, at the same time being kept clean and not dying alone.

Ritual and Prayer

The hospice was established by a Catholic religious order whose members formed the Pastoral Care Team. Most patients and families who are admitted to this hospice would be familiar with and welcome Catholic tradition and practice, reflecting the religious values of the Mid- West community which the hospice serves. The type and amount of prayer seems to be determined by the family. "I said to my nephew's wife - you start the rosary and she started the rosary." The rosary is a litany of three separate prayers repeated in decades concerned with the earthly and celestial life cycle of Christ, traditionally said daily in every family and at the bedside of the dying.

Some families were delighted with the lit candle, the crucifix and the holy water on a little table "which for me being an old fashioned Catholic was lovely. It was just the old style sick room" They felt that the "lovely prayers" took a lot of the grief away, "you're concentrating on prayers and the deceased is just lying there and you know its good for him." Ritual and prayer, having their own little crucifix, candles and the rosary "all these things have their place. It's a good thing." For one family "we're not a religious family. But it was lovely on his last day, the day he was dying to have prayer."

The nurses are praised for knowing when to bring the lit candles and the crucifix "once he was unconscious because he would have been frightened." A Church of Ireland family experienced the dying as "beautiful, with a candle lighting, holding hands and praying." The doctor and nurse's roles overlapped with Pastoral Care. A family uses the word "beautiful" ten times to describe a bedside vigil with ten people and states "The candles, the prayers and the two lovely nurses. A lovely nurse said the prayer for the dying."

The Qualities of Staff

Much is said of the qualities of staff members. They appreciated the ready availability of nurses to respond to patient discomfort as perceived by the family. "they were straight away into her, making her as comfortable as they possibly could. They were marvellous to her, as if there was no one else in the hospital". "The doctors went out of their way to help her an awful lot." Some were frustrated by the doctor not being more precise as to how much time was left. "Its very difficult for medics to know. I kept saying that to all his children. Everybody expects the doctor to know."

Families observe the way the patient is treated and equally how they are treated. They liked the individual unobtrusive attention by a named nurse each day. They liked the easy access to the doctor "if you wanted to see a doctor, you saw a doctor and they gave you the time. They appreciated the time given to their needs. They understood the care that was being given because Dr K and Dr E would tell me "we've tried this today, it's not working, we tried that. Being treated as if we were the only family, being called by your first name and being treated as if you were the only person the doctor was dealing with," made a great difference to the families. They acknowledged that all staff were "so good", "down to the girls who do the cleaning". "The nurses, the doctors, the nuns were absolutely brilliant."

The attitude of the nurses of "total care, total focusing, totally zoned in on the person who was very ill" was praised. The relatives comment on the "professionalism and attention to detail "of the night nurse. They valued "the total respect of the person" The kitchen staff would make tea and put aside meals for the family at night. Even the cleaners coming in and out, knowing everybody, saying hello. Pastoral Care, "like a mother", would bring up the dinner from the kitchen. The priests also visited, praying and spending a long time with them.

Some appreciated that the doctor sought them out every day to explain very clearly what the relatives needed to know and to assure them, "they were looking for you instead of you trying to find them"

Other families perceived that they had to "hunt for the doctors, it was hard to talk to doctors, not getting straight answers."

Families liked being treated as individuals "not like you're kind of a number and you don't matter". Families previous experiences of interactions with health professionals combined with the intensity of this emotional situation may predetermine how they react to this experience of death. Communication needs to be direct and finely tuned. A nurse advised a son that his Dad was low but "I didn't know what low meant really: a little bit down, sleepy? I didn't realise he was going to die." Any deviation from this intensive attention is remembered by the family. They were less comfortable if at the time of dying unfamiliar nurses were on duty. They were uncomfortable when the new nurses said "it is time" and the family had not noticed the imminence of death. Communication-on-demand describes the accessibility of staff to the families. For this reason alone a high staff to patient ratio must reflect the intensity of care expected by families. "Availability of somebody there to talk about it all the time was the greatest comfort." One woman recognises that this intense support prior to her mother's death would help her in her bereavement "after the death I felt I had done all I could, nothing left unsaid."

At the moment of death, families observe and remember the care in great detail. They value professionalism and courtesy. They need direct and regular communication. This is summarised in a sisters description of the care of her dying brother:

"The nurses and doctors, this is what I love for the onlooker, the dignity they bestow on patients, this is all I ever heard "Frank, how are you?" the kindness and dignity.......".

The Specialist Palliative Care Unit

The experience of the moment of death is reflected in the family's overall experience of care in the Palliative Care Unit. The family felt welcomed in the SPCU. One lady's dying mother "loved it here". Some preferred the four bedded ward to a "stuffy" single room. Another lady felt so safe that she would not go out even for an hour in the car. A husband was monitored so beautifully but "he hated the pictures on the wall". Some were distressed meeting other families and hearing their problems. It was wonderful care to have a bed and shower for family members. Despite many families being on the Palliative Care Unit, they described it as full of "quietness, calmness and peacefulness." Many relatives had a prior perception of the "hospice" as a place of suffering and of painful deaths. They were pleasantly surprised to find the Palliative Care Unit as a homely, cheerful place with peaceful surroundings and their relative comfortable and pain-free. "It was a home away from home." They appreciated being able to stay all day after the death "there was no rush to get us out of the way." One family describe how much this meant to them, "He died at twenty past two and we were here 'til eleven o' clock the next morning. There was no rush on us....they left him in the bed, they didn't take him out. There was no rush, we could have stayed all day......that was a big thing to us. It was nice to have that time with him, just ourselves."

Although they thought the death was beautiful, others were still glad that "his brain was altered, he came in here not knowing he was here." While the family was struggling with his admission, the patient "had a big smile waving at us". A patient had to travel for treatment elsewhere "the few days we were away, I couldn't wait to be back here, we'd be safe. There's a safeness in it." Another family mentions feeling "just so safe". Families had "the run of the place" with the patient "happy to be here" describing it as "a beautiful place, definitely not a sad place." A patient wanted to go to the SPCU as it "was like a five star hotel, not a depressing place".

The entire surroundings with no restrictions, no designated times, relatives able to stay at night, no hospital smell, created a "sense of peace." A family are grateful for this special place where their mother "was perfectly happy." The daughter had tried to provide care at home and was apprehensive about letting her mother go to the hospice. A patient welcomed the opportunity to go to the SCPU as "it was too much for us to look after her at home".

Sometimes relatives recalled negative memories of the death of a family member in the acute hospital. She felt that if her aunt had been in a hospice she would have had "more privacy" and "respect". She felt the candles and prayers in the hospital was" rushed" and "just a formality".

The faith of the dying person and how they lived as setting the tone of the final deathbed scene

The faith of the dying person and how they lived their lives is reflected in the deathbed scene and its rituals. The family said prayers and allowed candles and crucifix in ritual as this was their dying relatives wish. One son describes how his mother "was a great one for prayer….. it helped her all her life" and so prayer was used to comfort her at death. The family are familiar with the dying persons spiritual needs by the knowledge of how they lived. At one point a family states that 'only one decade of the rosary was said instead of five decades, at the bedside of their father, because "if he was there himself, he'd say "one decade is enough."

Others demonstrated this by saying how "Deep down he had a great faith, I think he believed he was going to a better place." And how "Joe'd be down on his knees in the morning… like he'd always bless himself at night and say his few prayers." Another family state how "He used to say his rosaries. He would fix rosary beads and send them out to the missions. He was a very spiritual man…….. he was a good man."

Another family member recognizes the mutual bond of faith, particularly when their loved one is so close to death:

"A few times particularly when I was on my own with her I'd say "would you like to pray?" and she'd say, "I'd like that" and that was a very good thing for her as much as it was for me."

The day before she died, in her humility Maureen reached out to her family and asked them to pray for her:

"It was morning before she said "kneel down there [at the bedside] and pray for me"… and we did."

Colm, Maureen's husband describes the unique relationship formed between his dying wife and the young doctor, who prayed with her a few days before her death:

"You prayed with her yourself, the three of us together. It was lovely. She thought it was lovely. She thought you were special……."

Rose, his sister, explains how Eddie reaffirms his faith close to death:

"He said you know I haven't been to church in ages, I haven't had communion in ages……so they [pastoral care] gave him a tiny bit of the communion. One night as I was leaving he said Rose, you forgot [to use] the holy water."

The dying person's death was acted out in the same way as how they lived as a continuum of life and death. I demonstrate the stages of death in Fig 6.2 to demonstrate the journey of the patients in this study on the moment of death. In my role as researcher, I usually met the patient and their relatives in the stage of acceptance of death. The reason for this was that the patient and their relatives seemed more open to talk with me and willing to be included in the study after they had reached this stage of acceptance. This was usually a time of great sadness but with it also a came a sense of calm and peace. One family was an exception to this. As I introduced myself to this family three weeks before their father died, they were very angry. This anger lessened over the next few weeks but persisted until the death of their father and afterwards. The family seemed to be in the early stages of acceptance but anger was still present. As discussed with the palliative care team, it seemed there were many issues still unresolved within the family.

Fig 6.2

"Stages of dying"

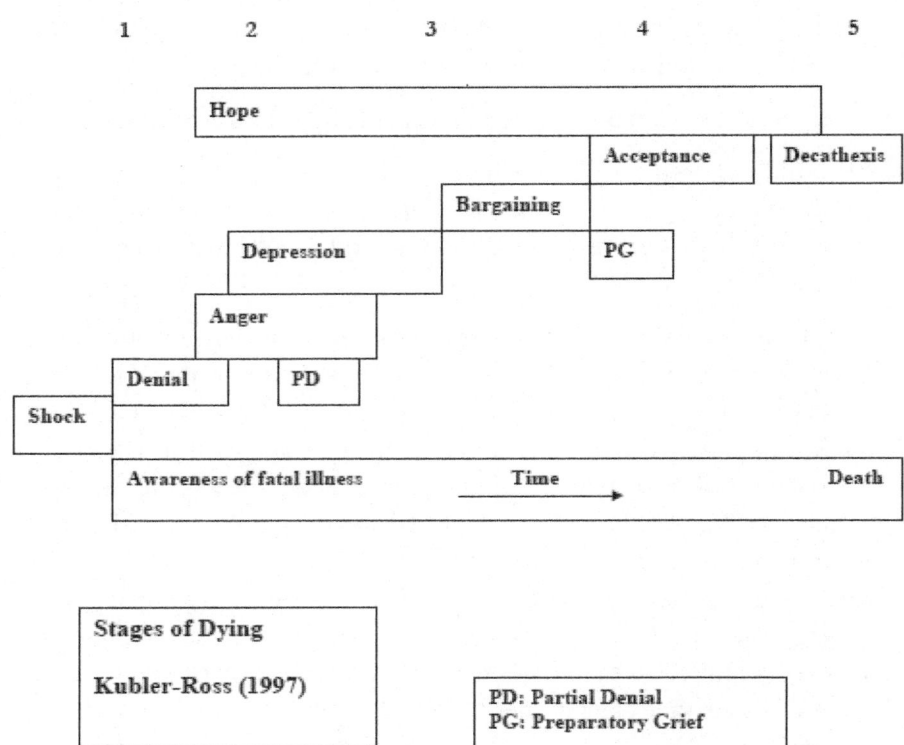

As in the diagram shown in Fig 6.2, hope still exists through all the stages of dying even to death. This is usually expressed in the relatives by the hope they have that the patient will receive all the appropriate care and also the hope of comfort and pain relief. The dying person hopes for peace and comfort and both patient and relatives can find hope and acceptance through their spiritual beliefs.

Dying person waiting for someone or for a blessing

A son describes how his dying mother is going to wait for the arrival of his brother at her deathbed:

" Mother's going to wait for Larry to come home. Don't ask me how she's going to do it but she's going to do it for Larry."

The same man describes his sisters arrival from London at his mother's bedside.

"Fiona said to her, if she didn't say it once she said it twenty times, "Mother, Ann-Marie's here." After a long time, it must have been a supreme effort, mother said, "I know".

A dying mans sister describes how her brother seems to wait for a blessing before he dies:

"There was a little cross on the tray and then he had his own that we brought in and a candle. Sister said one of the prayers and you'd swear he hung on til he got that blessing in the end. He just took a few gasps and then died."

A farmer describes his wife waiting for a blessing from the parish priest:

[Maureen] went into unconciousness about ten o'clock in the morning...... she was waiting for someone, we thought. We thought she was waiting for Sr Anne, but at five thirty [pm], the local parish priest came in and gave her absolution and the blessing again.... she was on her way then, she was waiting for that."

Love and respect shown for the dead body
Of significance in the study is the love and respect shown by the family, not only for the dying person but also for the dead body. There is beauty in the dead person. The sister of a dying man says "he was lovely to be with, a lovely aura. 'Twas like as if he was asleep. A beautiful expression on his face."

Another man describes his dead mother: "She was a beautiful corpse." A nephew describes the calmness in the room while keeping vigil with his aunt's body, "Even when Nora passed away and we were in the room, I felt at ease."

An elderly couple lovingly describe their son laid out in his coffin:

"If you had seen him laid out..... looked lovely and .... a smile. Everyone said it. But he was smilin'. Oh, you'd love to look at him. And the children... we brought them over privately and they kissed him and felt him and everything."

There is no fear in these descriptions, only an extension of love and consolation even after death.

Humour

Humour often featured in the stories of these recently-bereaved people. Two of the amusing stories involved the hospital bed, in particular the mattress. A few minutes after their mother died, the mattress was still "pumped up" and plugged in and as it moved M thought her mother was still alive. As they were giggling over this, their brother arrived and decided to pull the plug with the result that their mother started moving again. Once again the mattress re-inflated with their mother inside as Pat re- inserted the plug, "I mean it was the strangest thing. She would have had a laugh herself." Pastoral care brought three or four candles into the room as MOD was dying. Her daughter remarked "None of them would light. The fourth light. Was she keeping it out so she could have a bit longer!"

As they gathered around the bed waiting for the expected death they were telling humorous stories of exploits in their youth remarking to the unconscious patient "Listen Joe, you're hearing things now... you've never heard before!" Frank loved a joke and after he died, his son in law came in remarking "Isn't that bed making an awful noise". So Ann sitting nearest the wall pulled the plug. "Didn't the bed go down and poor Frank was sinking in the bed. He'd have laughed and said, "Holy God what are they doing to me now!" In the midst of our grief he started deflating inside of it!"

Chapter 7:
Field-notes, Interviews and Conclusions

Field-Notes: Introduction

The following are excerpts of field-notes I wrote down by hand after each interview in my research. These field-notes, though describing interviews of similar format, highlight the uniqueness and individuality of each of my encounters with a bereaved family. They demonstrate the variation in the families' needs and understanding, the emotional stages of their grief and how I as researcher and interviewer had to learn to accommodate, to facilitate and be sensitive to the families wishes at all times.

CB

I interviewed Mr and Mrs B in their home, whose 35 year old son, CB had died in the SPCU:

I went to interview Mr and Mrs B the parents of CB who had died in the SPCU 10 days earlier. They lived in a poor estate on the edge of the city. Their house stood in part of a tiny row of houses behind the large Cathedral. Their house was part of a cul-de-sac. I recognized Mrs B waiting at the door with her two grandchildren (CB's children, two little girls). The children were on their way out to meet their mother. Their fathers funeral had been a few days earlier. I entered the small house and walked into the small sitting room on the left. Mr B sat by the fire. I expressed by condolences to them both, as Mrs B sat next to her husband and I sat on a chair opposite.

I explained about the tape-recorder and all about the interview. Mrs B was very interested and asked many questions about the tape-recorder. Mrs B began to speak first. She said that CB had a peaceful death and she expressed appreciation at all the care her son was given. She was very grateful to all the people that came to the funeral and brought food and drink to the house. Then the tape-recorder started to act up. I had spent a half-hour prior to coming setting it correctly, ensuring it was recording at the proper volume, now it was recording at a lower volume and not picking up Mr B's voice which was very low. I didn't want to cause much fuss as I felt Mr and Mrs B might get uncomfortable, but it worked out well as Mrs B did most of the talking. I felt Mrs B was putting on a brave face as she talked a lot but seemed to hide her terrible grief and sadness. Both spoke lovingly about their grandchildren and how brave they were at the funeral. They were pleased at the large attendance at the funeral and praised the staff at the hospice.

The sadness of the home lingered with me for a while afterwards and the stories of the courage of the children. CB was Mr and Mrs B's only child and their loss was profound. Sometimes I wondered why they would give time to talk to me in the midst of their deep sorrow, however I began to understand that I could share some stories with them of my visits to CB over the previous few months which in this simple act might provide consolation.

CT

Mr D was a middle-aged family man whose mother CT, had died two weeks earlier in the SPCU:

I met Mr D at the reception. He smiled immediately and began to talk about his mother CT who had died 2 weeks earlier in the SPCU. He struck me as an open and honest man. He spoke in the interview at length about his mother and also the death of his adopted son a few years earlier and how he and his wife had grieved so much. I found that Mr D seemed to want to talk and liked to talk. He loved to talk about his faith and how his mother had passed it on to him and all the family. He said he had a special devotion to a prayer called the Chaplet of Divine Mercy. The interview lasted 40 minutes.

Mr D finished the interview by asking could he have a copy of the tape for himself. I said I would ask my supervisor and then send him a copy when possible. I noted that this was the first time someone showed an interest in the recording which showed me once again to be always ready for the unexpected. On replaying the tape I thought that I seemed too quiet, that Mr D at times spoke over me as I asked the questions. However, despite this I noticed that all the questions were answered very well throughout the interview.

HJ
I met with Mrs. P. and her daughter K in the SPCU for the interview:

This was going to be my second interview for the study. I was a bit nervous. How would it go? Would the family be too upset to talk? Would the tape-recorder work? There were a long list of possible problems.

I met with Mrs P and her daughter K at the front door. I thanked them for coming in so soon after the death of HJ, their husband and father. Mrs P looked very upset. I signaled to them if they'd like to sit down and have a cup of coffee in the little alcove off the foyer. They said they'd like that. Mrs P expressed her distress at returning to the hospice where her husband had died. I listened and said that if it was too much for her we didn't have to do the interview, but she said she'd like to.

I had arranged to use an interview room upstairs near the SPCU. As it was my first interview it never dawned on me to use my own office downstairs. It was only when Mrs P said she did not want to go near the ward where her husband died that I realized my downstairs office would be the best place. It worked out very well.

K did most of the talking. Mrs P was finding it difficult. She was not relaxed. Her daughter said she might like a cigarette, so I said she could have one in the room, no problem. I opened a window and Mrs P became more relaxed and smiled. Mrs P spoke a little more after that. The topic of the moment of death was difficult and emotional for Mrs P as she said she wasn't there and that upset her greatly. Overall K answered most of the questions and answered them very well.

The circumstances surrounding the interview weren't very smooth, but the interview itself went well. I told Mrs P and her daughter that they did extremely well and thanked them for their effort to come. They replied by saying that it was the least they could do for all the care HJ was given by the staff in the hospice. I learnt from this interview that flexibility and intuition are needed at all times, in all situations by the researcher.

HH

Mrs. H's brother had died in the SPCU and her daughter J came also for the interview:

I met Mrs. H, and J her daughter at the door of the hospice. I had not expected J and had not met her before. I learnt that as a researcher that you had to accommodate to the unexpected at an instant and accept readily any sudden change of plan. G, their brother, and their uncle (respectively), had died in the SPCU. I had spoken to Mrs. H on the phone explaining the interview and the use of the tape-recorder. We walked to my office and talked on the way. Mrs. H discussed how difficult it had been since her brother had died, how she missed calling to him every day like she used to. Once we had reached the office and settled in, I explained about the tape recorder as I had done previously on the phone to Mrs H. J however seemed more aware of the tape-recorder and self-conscious while speaking. To my surprise both began to be critical of CG's care in the SPCU.

I noticed my negative reaction to this as I had been lulled into a comfortable position through previous interviews by constant praise of the SPCU. They both seemed annoyed but as the interview proceeded they began to praise his overall care. I felt the interview went well and that they needed to talk and voice their concerns and irritations. I walked them to the door and thanked them for their help and for coming in.

CG

Mrs R. and her son D met me at the reception desk to speak with me about their uncle, GC, who had died in the SPCU. It definitely was not the easiest of interviews:

I met with Mrs R and her son D, a man in his early thirties. At once on meeting them at the reception, I felt uncomfortable. One of the main reasons for this, was the young mans first question in a commanding tone "Are you the consultant?" I explained that I was not, to which he replied "I thought we were meeting the consultant". My first impressions were that this man was going to be difficult and I was right.

The conversation became stilted as I explained the format of the interview and its purposes. I said that I had explained this previously on the ward and by phone to Mrs R, to which she nodded, but this didn't seem to lessen his angry tones. I showed them the information sheet and the consent form. D sat in silence reading it for five minutes before saying "I suppose no one says 'no' to signing this." I said he didn't have to sign it if he didn't want to. They proceeded to sign the form.

The interview went smoother than expected after D had asked "How long will this take?"

After the interview was over as I walked them both along the long corridor to the front door, D asked "Are you a doctor?" I said I was and he said he wanted to see were we keeping to the rules on the information sheet. D was still annoyed even after the interview no matter how much placation and explanation I had given. I am still learning how not to take people's anger personally in their grief and try not to react to it as a researcher and interviewer.

QE
Mr T's wife, QE had died a few weeks previously in the SPCU and I interviewed him in my office in the SPCU:

I had arranged over the phone to meet with Mr. T at the reception desk of the SPCU. On the phone he was a little tearful when I said that it must be hard for him on the death of his wife a few weeks earlier. We arranged to meet the following day.

After we met we walked towards a small office on the first floor as my office was in use. On the way we met two doctors. Both had a few words with Mr. T. To them Mr. T described his wife QE's last few moments. He wanted to know "was the fact she smiled at him, all in his head or what?"

We went into the small office on the first floor which had two windows facing out onto a small courtyard. There were a few small plants on the windowsill, a small table where I placed my tape-recorder and a small picture frame of St. Pio. I started the interview and switched on the tape-recorder. Mr T's voice was a little low and muffled, so I had to check was his voice recording. We then continued. He spoke of his wife's QE's death, about the family and the time of death. He praised the hospice and the doctors and nurses. Several interruptions came in the course of the interview by a few knocks on the door. They did not interfere with the Mr. T's overall flow of conversation. He repeated many times that he felt his wife was around him all the time and then when he turned around she was not there. I felt that they must have been a very close couple and loved each other very much.

On listening to Mr. T. he described his wife QE as having gone through a spiritual crisis a few days before she died. He described her conflict between the old traditions of her beliefs and the new. E questioned a few days before her death where she was going after she died and what about all the scandals in the church, what was she to believe. He said this caused her great distress.

BB

Mr. B met me at the front door of the SPCU, several weeks after his wife, BB had died. I interviewed him in my office: On meeting Mr. B he struck me as a warm open man. The moment we met he spoke openly about his wife who had died a few weeks before. During the interview he became tearful on describing his wife's death. What emerged from his descriptions was a strong love for his wife and his deep faith in God.

Mr. B described his wife, as a wonderful person and a woman of great faith, with a love of God and her family. He said the family never lost hope in a cure or healing of her illness and they kept hoping and trusting in God till the end. Mr. B mentioned how his wife had looked after her own parents until they died and then his own parents as well as himself and the children. He said she could have worked outside the home but chose not to so she could look after the family.

The interview lasted 30 minutes. Mr. B found it too difficult to answer the questions relating to the moment of death of his wife. Some answers were very short to those questions and it was difficult to get any detail. I understand this as this topic is so emotional and sensitive that the interviewee can only express so much in their grief and it is important for the interviewer to be aware of this, to reassure the person and know when to end the interview.

Mr. T did not speak about his own faith but said that he was pleased that one of the nurses prayed the rosary for his wife at the end. Afterwards I felt I could have asked more on the topic of his own faith but Mr. T seemed tired so we ended the interview.

It seemed he had said all he wanted to say and asked the questions he had wanted to ask. I walked Mr. T to the front door and thanked him for coming in. He said he hoped we'd meet again.

Some Conclusions
The themes presented in this qualitative enquiry into the moment of death comprise: the detailed description of dying, the vigil and importance of being present, mutual giving between patient and their relatives, the qualities of the staff, the value of ritual and prayer and the open environment of the Specialist Palliative Care Unit. In all interviews the moment of death is marked by presence, individually and silently and in community. Total attention is given by family and staff to each person and prayer is ritualized in words and candles. It is a moment to be witnessed and is part of a long and t old tradition of an expression of love of which the palliative care staff grow to understand. There is an art in being able to stand quietly by, an art achieved by the doctors and nurses and other staff members. At the moment of death families observe and remember this care in great detail. At the same time they wish to feel safe. They need ready support accessibility and communication with professional staff. The purpose of my research and this dissertation is to show as Ellershaw (2003) holds, that the function of specialist palliative care is to disseminate high quality care to dying patients. At the same time the dissemination of this care requires that the public and carers - both actual carers and potential carers, lay and professional, be informed of the needs and wishes of the dying and their families at the moment of death. This close look at what it is like to die, is the equivalent of learning anatomy to understand the living physical body. I have

attempted to dissect the moment of death in order to help others, families and patients alike to face that moment themselves. I have not used instruments (Mayland 2008) to examine this critical time, rather I have dissected the eye witness accounts of astute and empathetic observers.

One family stated that all was not peaceful when estranged family members met together at the bedside of a dying relative. Some relatives had travelled from afar to the bedside of their dying relative after leaving that relative in anger and haste many years before. Returning relatives can still harbor resentments and anger many years later both towards the dying relative and family members. The holistic therapeutic care given by members of the professional palliative care team to both patient and family is highlighted at this time, providing the emotional and psychological support required by the patient and their family, assuaging the conflict and encouraging the dialogue required for interrelationship healing.

Of note during the study were the emotions revealed at the interviews. The emotions varied between anger, sadness, acceptance and calmness, indifference, detachment and depression. For no expressed reason, at times, relatives reacted angrily, possibly due to the depth of their grief, 1-6 weeks after the death of their relative, when the interviews took place. In one family consisting of a mother and three teenagers, the children remained silent throughout the interview as their mother spoke. At times I, as the interviewer, found it difficult to accept this expression of anger but on discussion of the situation with my supervisor I learnt to become more objective lest it affect my perception of the family. All families reacted favorably to the study itself and said they were glad to be part of the study that aimed to improve the care of the dying and their relatives.

Study Limitations: Selection of participants
I noticed bias in my initial selection of participants at the beginning of the study, in my negative reactions to certain families, who were hostile and unwelcoming. As referred to previously, one particular

family were angry and difficult with myself and staff. As a researcher, I found communication with them difficult and I was unsure whether the family were genuinely unsuitable for inclusion in the study or whether I was over- reacting and putting my own feelings between myself and the family. I discussed the situation with my supervisor and made field-notes and recordings in a personal diary.

It was the recording and re-reading of my field-notes and personal diary, that helped me to restore my objectivity and to recognize my reaction for what it was- a natural reaction to a hostile atmosphere. I persisted on visiting the family and their ill father and gradually, the family became more communicative after several visits and after the death of their father, agreed to an interview in their home. The family provided an in-depth interview, enriching the overall results of the study. This demonstrated to me, as a researcher, that my initial emotional reaction to an unpleasant situation was misleading and created a biased view. These situations which produce a biased reaction, provide a challenge for us, as researchers, but with reflection, discussion and persistence, when surmounted, can provide positive and enriching results.

There is also the real possibility of bias in selecting a small sample, in which a wide range of informants are used in order to select key informants with access to important sources of knowledge (Mays & Pope, 1995 (a)). The idea of this type of sampling is not to generalize to the whole population but to indicate common links or categories shared between the setting observed and others like it. At its most powerful, the single case can demonstrate features or provide categories relevant to a wide number of cases as is applicable to the selection process in this study. Although the sample selected was small each family in the study represents a single unique story and each patient reveals in turn more information, forming a composite picture which encompasses the moment of death in the Palliative Care Unit. Each patient and family demonstrated features and providing categories relevant to the general population. The study sample might appear to over-represent the adult population as there were no children as patients in this study. The supervisor and I decided that the involvement of children and their families would require a separate study, an area for future research. As it happened, in this study, 3 teen-age participants were included as part of one family interviewed during this study.

Setting confined to one Specialist Palliative Care Unit.

Some critics might ask - why the study did not take place in several different Palliative Care Units. As this study took place in the only large specialist palliative medical department in the Mid-Western region of Ireland, I considered it sufficient to have a representative sample of 20 patients and their families in this single Palliative Care Unit without including the few outreach services sub-units in the region. Since the aim of this study is the experience of the moment of death in a Specialist Palliative Care Unit, a representative sample is provided for this setting of choice.

As the aim of qualitative research is to watch people and events and to find out about diverse behaviours and interactions in their natural settings, qualitative observation takes place in a natural setting not in an experimental one (Mays & Pope, 1995 (b)), as does this present qualitative study of the moment of death in a Specialist Palliative Care Unit, providing a true representation of the moment of death specific to this setting.

Potential Interview Bias

I exercised great care in avoiding bias due to direct personal questioning or by leading questions. According to Spradely (1979), a semi-structured format allows openness to changes of sequence and forms of questions in order to follow up the answers given and the stories told by the subjects. Bias was minimized by keeping questions from me the researcher to a minimum confining them to questions of clarification and by allowing the family member to freely express their thoughts, feelings and actions.

Not seeking specific answers to questions, I waited for the emergence of the heretofore un-spoken or un-thought of question retrospectively revealed by the spontaneous reflection or observation made by the patient's relative. At no time was it ever suggested by me to relatives that the purpose of the interview was to obtain their opinions of the treatment or management of the deceased relative.

Bias in Data analysis

As researcher, I was fully aware of any bias as the study proceeded. My field-notes, (as shown in Chapter 7) and diary acted as guides to any developing bias or over-reaction on my part, either positive or negative, towards people and situations that would directly or indirectly influence the results of the study. The purpose of keeping these accounts was to help in the analysis of the study as it progressed, by conferring with my supervisor about difficulties encountered and discussing any noticeable biased views on my part that might alter my collection and analysis of the data to date.

The nature of its setting in a Specialist Palliative Care Unit under the care of the Catholic order of nuns, The Little Company of Mary, might constitute a reason for this study being considered bias that might affect overall data analysis. The people of the Mid-West of Ireland are primarily of the Catholic faith. - 17 of the 20 families participating, were of the Catholic faith (without special selection), 2 families were of the Church of Ireland denomination, 1 family were agnostic and I, as researcher belong to the Catholic faith. Rituals, prayers and expressions in this study are predominantly Catholic. Nevertheless, I was conscious that my unfamiliarity with a non-Catholic tradition might render this study skewed as not representing society as a whole. This fact may also give the impression that this study is not representative of society as a whole as there are many cultures and traditions in Ireland at present and this study is confined to the Christian tradition. However, I believe that the fact the Specialist Palliative Care Unit is predominantly of the Catholic or Christian tradition does not detract from the overall aim of the study in addressing the needs of dying patients and their families. Death and dying are universal themes. Due to the universality of death, the results encountered in this study can be applied to many diverse cultures and traditions throughout the world.

I discussed with my supervisor at length any tendency to bias on my part, due to unfamiliarity with Church of Ireland and agnostic traditions. We noted that as I had reacted openly to all traditions, that these issues were not of significance and would not affect the study in any way. I also noted, on comparison of the interviews between the Catholic families and the Church of Ireland and agnostic families that there were no differences in the themes expressed and issues raised surrounding the moment of death of their relatives. The non-Catholics use or lack of use of rituals and prayer might have been different but their expressions of the need for dignity, privacy, a sense of community and presence, accompaniment, love and affection, mutual caring and trust in the professional and lay carers were similar. A Church of Ireland family recounted the following experience:

"The hospice chaplain came in and put his hand on Dad's head and he held my hand and I held my daughters and we said our prayers and he went out and our rector came in and he did exactly the same......it was a beautiful experience for my daughter and I, absolutely beautiful."

The same family recalled that there was no crucifix at the bedside but they had candles:

"[There were] candles, yes..... [at the bedside]..... people light a candle for hope don't they or for a wish for peace in troubled times...."

A Catholic family who said that they were not religious but agnostic, recount how their dying father was very comfortable:

"We're not a religious family and he [dying father] wasn't...... we're not church goers..... but it [prayer] was lovely on the last day, the day he was dying, because he appreciated it then that day. Oh, at death, I think his family whipped him off, they came for him. It was a happy time even though we knew he was dying. I've seen people die before and to me it was very peaceful."

"Everybody was very good, it made us comfortable. We had a room, we had a shower....it was brilliant ...... no one made us feel that we shouldn't be there. We were made feel quite comfortable."

This Study: Research Strengths

This study is unique in that interviews were performed with bereaved families as short as 1 week after the death of a relative which allowed the clear and vivid recall of accounts of the moment of death by relatives in a profound and intimate way. Peruse of the literature to date has failed to reveal such a detailed account of the moment of death after death.

A true, vivid and accurate account of the moment of death From the qualitative nature of a study such as this, all accounts of the moment of death are direct quotes from relatives. These direct quotes are used throughout the findings of the study, portraying a true, accurate and moving account of what happens at the time of dying and the effect it has and the impression it indelibly makes on the close relatives of the dying person.

Of benefit to the participants

I found that patients and families were eager to participate in the study and were enthusiastic to tell their stories. Repeatedly emphasized was their wish to help future patients and their families by their own participation in the study and by their willingness and determination from the onset of the study to be interviewed by me. These families also discussed with me after the interview, how they found the interview of help to them in their grief.

Provide incentives for future research

This study will empower health professionals for the future in their care of the dying, by providing new and fresh insights into the needs of dying patients and their families. This study will also provide new vignettes and further incentives for bereavement research into care of the dying, in different environments and with participants from varied health settings.

It is hoped that, this study on the moment of death, while contributing to future studies on care of the dying and their families, will lead to a new departure in health care, in management and medical practice and in medical education, where care of the dying patient will become as important a focus as care of the "living", particularly in the acute hospital setting, in which it is sadly lacking at present.

Further education at undergraduate and postgraduate levels

This qualitative enquiry in a Specialist Palliative Care Unit can be another teaching tool at both undergraduate and postgraduate levels, education of medical doctors, nurses, social workers, chaplains, psychologists and psychiatrists and particularly in the speciality of palliative care, by providing insight into the sensitivity and dignity of care of the dying for the patient and their families.

"Expecting the unexpected": The need to obviate the small but important practical problems at interview

1. Initially, I used a small Marantz tape-recorder with its static in-built microphone to interview a small number in a small room. The arrival of a greater number of family members than arranged (including teenagers) illustrated the need not only for a mobile microphone or lead extension but also the need for a standby interview room.

This is illustrated by the following extract from my diary of an interview with a wife of a man who had died in the SPCU two weeks previously and their three teenage children.

"Mrs. E always struck me as a gentle, open person. I had met her on many occasions on the ward with her dying husband. On this occasion Mrs. E had agreed to do the interview with me in my office downstairs from the SPCU.

I met her at the reception desk and at once was surprised to see that three teenagers were with her. I had not met them before and Mrs. E introduced me to them as her children hoping they could accompany us in the interview. I immediately stated that is was no problem at all but as I walked with them to the interview room I began to think of whether I would have enough chairs, whether the Marantz tape-recorder might not have a recording range for all the children and whether the interview itself would be too much for them. Meanwhile, I asked Mrs. E how she was coping. She said it was difficult as she still could not believe her husband had died but she was fine to do the interview.

We reached the office. I only had to get one other chair. Noone wanted a cup of tea. Mrs. E and the children were silent as I explained about the recorder. I felt a little self-concious that there were so many people in the room. When Mrs E spoke with a soft gentle voice I wondered would her voice carry. With these potential problems mounting I felt the sooner the interview progressed the better.

Mrs. E spoke as the children sat in silence shifting in their chairs, except for the eldest girl who joined in with her mother now and again. I knew they were going through a difficult time and here they were in a small room listening to a recount of their father's death. It was very hard for them and I became more self-conscious and aware of their discomfort.

Mrs. E eased my discomfort by speaking at length and answering my occasional question very well, giving detailed accounts of her feelings and attitudes to the illness and death of her husband and praising the care her husband received at all stages of his illness. As soon as the interview was over I thanked them all for coming in and guided them to the canteen and felt slightly relieved that it was over."

2. No matter how well-tested or frequently-tested beforehand, electronic failure in the recorder occurred. This was not only a cause of frustration but much more importantly a cause of much greater inconvenience to the mourning families who may have travelled for many hours for my interview as illustrated in my field-notes in Chapter 7.

3. Various levels of anger can be expected when interviewing bereaved families. The following is an extract from my fieldnotes on visiting Mrs. P's house one week after her husband's death:

"I travelled to Mrs. P's home. The housing estate had a dishevelled appearance and most of the houses looked rundown. I found Mrs. P's house eventually. It was an unassuming house at the end of a row of houses in a cul-de-sac.

On answering the door Mrs. P looked worn and tired. She invited me into her home into the living room. A young pretty fair-haired girl, Mrs. P's daughter, offered me a cup of tea. I accepted gratefully. I sympathized with them both on the loss of their husband and father respectively. I had heard and had experienced myself on meeting the family once before in the SPCU that they were "difficult to deal with". For this reason I was initially uncomfortable.

I went over once again with the family, as I had explained previously in the SPCU, the purpose of my visit to their home, the interview and the use of the tape recorder. Mrs. P signed the consent form. As I switched on the tape recorder, Mrs. P spoke of the loss of her husband. As she spoke her daughter returned with tea and biscuits.

Mrs. P's daughter D too began to speak - forcefully and with anger - while laughing intermittently - about members of staff who had attended her father in the SPCU. D dismissed members of staff as inept and of no help to her father or the family. I sat there and said little. I found it difficult as I knew each member of the staff well and knew how hard they had worked and had cared for Mr P.

......Mrs. P and her daughter continued to speak of the days and weeks before Mr. P's death. They said that at Mr. P's death his family "whipped him off" that "they came for him" and they felt that he was talking to his dead sister before he died. The daughter said that in her dreams she saw his dead sister come up in a black car, but she never opened the garden door, so she didn't come in. Then she said the knocking started at the door at home every morning at six o' clock. Mrs. P stated that her husband did" the rounds" when he was in the coma, that he went to back to all the places that he loved......"

The above was one of the many varied reactions I encountered in my interviews for this study. Some families were accepting and simply sad, one to six weeks after death of their relative, others expressed their anger at the death of their relative. I as, interviewer initially found being at the receiving end of this anger difficult but I learned that as the interview progressed the relatives' anger lessened and essentially all the participants commented that they were glad they had the opportunity to talk about their grief.

4. The need for sensitivity and accommodation by the researcher to the needs and wishes of the interviewee.

Sometimes the interview does not proceed exactly according to schedule and it is important that the needs of the interviewee always come first. In one interview, an elderly man who had lost his wife two weeks before, met me at the door stating that first of all he wanted to go to Mass with his daughter in the little chapel in our Palliative Care Unit. I joined them and three of us went to Mass for the next 30 minutes. (See Chapter 7 on field-notes.)

Another young man whose father had died in the Palliative Care Unit a few weeks before, wanted to first visit the ward where his father had died. Immediately we went to the room where his father had died and where his son had spent the many months with him prior to his death. There he met with and talked to the doctors and nurses who had treated his father, which afterwards he said was of great help to him.

I learnt from this episode that what is said and that which happens in the interview room is not confined to this place alone. It extends into the days, weeks and months prior to that day, through daily contact between myself and the families in a mutual bond of trust, at the bedside of their dying relative. The following is an example from field-notes I recorded, on my visit to the home of the wife and sister of N who had died two weeks previously in the SPCU. This extract which demonstrates that accommodating to the unexpected can lead to fruitful results. "I had arranged previously by phone with K to call out to her house in S. I was surprised how well she seemed on the phone and how she was so open warm and friendly two weeks after her husband N's death. On my arrival at the house K answered the door and invited me in. It was a beautiful tidy, small house. I noticed how everything was perfectly coordinated and beautifully decorated. Pink was the predominant colour with pine wooden floors in the hall and sitting room. As K walked me to the sitting room she spoke of how she was feeling. We sat on the couch and K spoke about the family and how they were coping, of how the days were alright but that she found the nights hard. She kept thinking that N was out at work and would be home soon. As we started talking about N's death, I decided to switch on the tape-recorder. The next 15 minutes were spent trying to get the tape-recorder to work. I felt embarrassed and annoyed with myself as I had checked the tape-recorder before leaving the office. K sat patiently by my side as I wrestled with the machine. I was annoyed also that K had just started to talk naturally about the actual death of her husband and now the flow was interrupted.

Then the doorbell rang and. K introduced me to her sister-in-law, N's sister A. I thought not only does my tape-recorder not work but now there are two people to interview which I had not expected. Was I supposed to include both for interview when I had not prepared the second person? Would the inclusion of the K's sister-in-law, A, alter the format of the interview or should I arrange the interview with K another day.

As I was asking myself all these questions I was introduced to A, a very friendly outgoing lady who started to talk in a most natural way about N's death. From A's exuberance in wanting to speak about the death of her brother it seemed most natural to include her in the interview and my previous worries subsided. As A continued to talk, my tape-recorder suddenly started to work.

Both ladies spoke of the beauty of N's death. They described his death as serene and happy. Their descriptions of N to each other were comforting and full of love. I noticed the shared love and affection that these two people had for N and the ease to which they described this love so openly to me a stranger and to each other. I felt privileged to be present and to be allowed to share in their reminiscences and expressions of love and affection. The interview lasted 45 minutes. As this was my first interview I was tentative in knowing how long the interview should last and I also was aware that K was becoming tired. When I had turned the tape-recorder off, K offered me tea and cake.

On K's return, A spoke of her bitterness towards God in leaving some people behind while taking others. K then spoke of her strong faith and her belief that N was beside her and in heaven. On hearing this A remained silent. A spoke of her children, in how her son was a worrier like his father and that their daughter was not like that at all. K started to talk of her faith in St Thérèse of the Little Flower. How she had been praying to her and that the belief was that a rose was the sign she was looking after you. K described how when they came out N's room in the SPCU one day, there was a tray with a rose on its surface. At N's funeral Mass, the priest spoke of St Thérèse also. K said she felt very comforted by all of this as she felt N was now with St Thérèse. A. said that she was feeling a little depressed in the morning. I mentioned the bereavement counselor S in the SPCU, that I could arrange for her to meet with him but A said she would not be ready for that yet.

This had been my first interview for the study and I felt that it had gone well, despite the tape-recorder. Even though A was an unexpected visitor her presence greatly enhanced the richness of the interview and her contribution was most valuable adding a renewed dynamic to my visit. This demonstrated to me as a visitor and as a researcher that we must be ready for any interruptions and deviations to our plans as not everything goes to plan and that as we adjust to the unexpected the newfound plans can often prove to be better.

Families' wishes as expressed in this qualitative enquiry: This study on the moment of death has proved a positive and enriching experience for both relatives and for the dying person as their needs are listened to and fulfilled. Many are the reasons spoken of during the interviews with the family members as to why this is so. The relatives' wishes reflecting those of the dying were summarized from the interviews as follows:

1. Their dying relative being comfortable and free from pain.
2. The dignity of the dying person respected at all times. Thoughtfulness and compassion demonstrated by the simple acts of kindness in changing the clothes, combing the hair, maintaining the dryness, cleanliness and neatness of the dying patient.
3. Being allowed to stay the night with the dying person with access to meals nearby for as long as possible.
4. Maintaining the quietness, discretion and non- intrusion by professional carers at the most sensitive times. Knowing when to leave the family alone, allowing them to sit and grieve with the dead body.
5. Being offered a cup of tea at a difficult time.
6. Being able to pray with the dying person.
7. Being allowed to stay and maintain a family vigil day and night on the ward in the SPCU.
8. Being able to call on doctors, nurses and Pastoral Care at any time of the day or night.
9. Having silence and peacefulness in the SPCU, as starkly compared with the noise and intrusiveness of the acute hospital setting.
10. Being listened to by professional carers and being given time to express their concerns and needs.
11. Being allowed to sit with the dead body for as long as they wished immediately after death.
12. The absence of haste or rush before or after the death of the patient and maintaining a quiet atmosphere of calmness at these times.

Incentives for future research

From this qualitative enquiry into the moment of death, I wish to re-emphasize how important it is to all carers, both lay and professional, to respond to the needs of the dying and their families at the moment of death. This study set in a Specialist Palliative Care Unit, provides a foundation and cornerstone for future research on the moment of death and I aim to continue this research in the following areas:

Further analysis of the relationship and interaction and needs of staff, relatives and patients at the moment of death. I would like to place more emphasis on the interaction of staff with the dying and their relatives and analyze qualitatively the staffs' perceptions, emotions and reactions to the moment of death.

This could be achieved by interviewing all individual staff members present at the death, matched with interviews with relatives of the same dead person who had been present also. This would provide a window into the moment of death through the eyes of staff and relatives at the same time. I would hope to compare-and-contrast staffs' and relatives' perceptions of the moment of death.

Further comparison of the moment of death in the acute hospital, Specialist Palliative Care Unit and in the home setting. The analysis of the moment of death of children and the experience of parents and professional staff, in the acute hospital, the home-setting and in the rare instances when a child's death occurs at present in the SPCU. This area of research would be particularly sensitive and would require a detailed review of ethical boundaries. However, it is an area largely unexplored to date.

Since this study explores the moment of death predominantly in the Catholic tradition and as Ireland is fast becoming a multicultural society, further research on the diverse cultural traditions of the moment of death would be of increasing importance for the future in acute hospitals, homes and SPCU.

Further Conclusions
My findings in this study on the moment of death in a Palliative Care Unit echo the findings of two previous studies where interviews of family members were used to analyze the moment of death. These include my previous published study on the moment of death in the home, (Donnelly, 2006) and that of Addington-Hall's (2001) use of surrogate or bereaved family member interviews to investigate the experiences of people at the end of life.

In my previous study (Donnelly, 2006) on death at home, the moment of death is described as intimate and the deathbed scene at home, described as "the gathering" with the dying patient and the main carer as being centre stage with professional carers' unobtrusive and moving off-stage. In this study, the choice of a Palliative Care Unit as a setting reverses the roles, where professional carers and the dying patient assume centrestage and family and relatives recede into the background. In both settings the bed itself becomes a metaphor representing intimacy and the reality of physical deterioration (Proot, 2004). Donnelly (2006) also suggests that caring for the dying at home allows the family carer to reach a place of more intense love, loneliness and expressed affection which is not reached when the dying person is in the Palliative Care Unit. On the other hand, this maybe not such a bad thing for some relatives, where the structure of a Palliative Care Unit reduces the ambient raw intensity of death at home, where the professionalism protects the mourning relative from intense emotion and grief, an act inaccessible and never before experienced during their life (Donnelly, 2006).

This is borne out by my observations during this study of the moment of death in the Palliative Care Unit. Though relatives expressed their willingness and preference to take care of their relative at home, they realized that they could not have managed at home both physically and emotionally. Family members were lavish in their praise of the care their relative received in the Palliative Care Unit and how wonderful it was that they could stay overnight if they wished and were provided with all the facilities they needed:

"They turned him, changed his clothes and washed him, like you know.... we were allowed to stay the night with him and all day, we had the run of the place, [we could] make tea when we wanted."

"Well, I had been looking after her at home, you know. I was always apprehensive was I doing the right thing. When she came to the hospice.... I'd leave perfectly happy..... she seemed so happy here. So, em it was a great comfort to have a place like this....'cos it really is a special place here."

For some relatives it is the realization that the care of their dying relative is not possible anymore and that the care provided by professionals and the Palliative Care Unit is a huge and welcome relief.

"Mom was putting a lot of pressure to come home. She really had this desire to be at home and Dad couldn't cope with the idea at all because he was so exhausted."

For others they could combine going home with care in the Palliative Care Unit:

"Yeah, he was very comfortable. He loved it in there, he did and he loved getting home as well. He loved the fact that he could come in and relax and get a bit of rest and go home again."

Addington-Hall (2001), states that the use of proxies or surrogates in after death interviews is valid from many previous studies (Ahmedzai, 1988; Cartwright, 1990; Higginson, 1994; Hinton, 1996; Field, 1995; Grassi, 1999). Arising from interviewing bereaved relatives and in the subsequent analysis of the data and the experience of the dying is the fact that the period between the experience and the recollection is crucial to the accuracy of the recalled information and the ease with which it is recalled (Baddley, 1990). The shorter the intervening period the easier the recall of information. It is for this reason in this moment of death study that, I interviewed relatives within 1-6 wks of death of their relative.

However, Addington-Hall (2001) warns us, that our need to interview relatives so soon after death must be balanced with the ethical concerns about upsetting relatives in their bereavement by what may be regarded as unnecessary intrusion into their grief arising from their unique moment in experiencing the enormity of death and with it the sense of loss which may be intense.

I concur with Valentine (2007), who in a previous study on the moment of death, involving interviews of 25 bereaved relatives in England, demonstrated how in a medicalized context, which emphasizes the biological nature of dying, these dying moments represent gestures of leave-taking in which elements lost to the medical discourse, but vital to making sense of mortality, were recovered: the spiritual, humanistic, social and emotional aspects of the dying experience.

What transforms dying moments into significant personal and social events is their reciprocal and shared nature (Donnelly, 2006; Kellehear & Lewin, 1988-1989). This reciprocity is very much evident in this study in the Specialist Palliative Care Unit, where mutual accompaniment at the death bed, involving both patient and relative, demonstrates gestures of love given through attention and embracing, by communication through facial expressions and sounds and also the simple act by the dying person of waiting for a travelling relative to reach the bedside. Mutual giving is very much part of leave taking and the final acts of farewell.

According to Kellehear & Lewin (1988-1989), at the most practical and interpersonal level, farewells tend to be times for the exchange of affection, reassurance and acceptance, with these interactions supplying reaffirmation and support to both patient and family. In these authors' study of 100 Australian dying patients many patients mentioned that merely to have their loved ones at the bedside would be a comfort and the goodbye would be embodied in looks and gestures rather than words.

Valentine (2007) re-affirms this by stating that these gestures of intimacy and relatedness signaled the dying persons imminent leave-taking. Kellehear & Lewin (1988-1989) summarise their findings by stating that farewells are an important way of reaffirming social bonds, of making dying a socially real and shared experience and of helping people to disengage. The qualities of holistic care are prevalent and reflected consistently throughout this moment of death study in a SPCU. Patients and family are tended to by lay and professional carers alike in a dignified manner, providing physical, social, psychological and spiritual care.

Only through this all-embracing care were patients and family ready and willing to become involved and contribute wholeheartedly to the moment of death study. Patients and their families expressed appreciation at the comfort and dignified care they received and expressed their gratitude at being able to express their wishes and needs through the interviews conducted. Though the aim of the study was not to promote hospice care in any particular way, but to define the moment of death through the eyes of relatives, their praise of the dignified holistic care given by health care professionals and all staff permeated the interviews during their descriptions of the moment of death. I concur with Ellershaw (2003) in so much as he states, that the function of specialist palliative care is to disseminate high quality care to dying patients, to have an advisory and educational role to influence the quality of care and that further education in palliative care needs to be targeted in both nursing and medical, undergraduate and postgraduate settings.

At the same time in addition to the high standard medical and nursing knowledge and care required in attending to the needs and requirements of the dying person and to the relatives and friends, I maintain that this is not enough. Essential also is the sensitivity and understanding of the palliative-carer to provide tactful, non-intrusive help, advice and guidance, based on understanding both learned and instinctive. These are essential qualities and not necessarily easily-applied. This is also true in the modern acute hospital setting where it is very difficult to acquire an appreciation for the great need for quietness to the point of stillness in the area of privacy that must be provided for the dying person and the grieving family members and friends. "I remember when we came in here [SPCU] the peace was the strongest...... I remember the very first night, the peace and the absence of trolleys clanging along the corridors. The trolleys come but you don't hear them."

This study has confirmed my initial premise that the moment of death is highly significant for the dying, their relatives and for professional carers and therefore there is greater urgency for us as healthcare professionals to focus on and examine this time of death in greater detail. We owe it to our patients and their families to dedicate our time and efforts in analyzing in close detail their needs and wants at this time.

Kellehear (1989), clearly states that without research with dying patients, the dying have no idea how others like them die and they want to know. When we become them, we may want to know too. Knowing how to provide comfort requires insight into the complete landscape of a dying patient's experience. Within the new horizons of palliative medicine, these insights will provide the foundation for novel and compassionate approaches intended to bolster hope enhance meaning and lessen suffering for patients nearing death (Chochinov 2006; Kastenbaum 1999). This study on the moment of death aims to achieve such a vision.

My role as a medical doctor and as a researcher in this study on the moment of death is unique. I assumed the role of nondirectional participation taking part in conversations and interviews with relatives and patients in an objective manner but without active intervention. I did not attend patients as a physician and although I had frequent visits with the patients before death, I was present only at the death of one patient at the request of the family. My supervisor and I felt it unnecessary and obtrusive to attend all deaths, but to attend those only when asked to by the families.

Initially, I was surprised at the family's natural friendliness and eagerness to include me in their visits to their dying relative on a regular basis. As I was included from the first day, it gave me an opportunity to speak with the dying person and their relative and to be included in all that took place at the bedside. Being with the family encouraged easy, direct, honest and open conversations with the dying and their families, nurturing a trusting, open relationship that followed through to deeper, richer and more fruitful research.

The findings and conclusions produced in this study emerged from the dying person's direct quotes as related to me by their relatives. They are direct expressions of the needs of the dying at the moment of their death. Their voices permeate this study illuminating and teaching us, showing us the way in how to nurture and care for the dying person and their relatives in the future. The use of interviews proved to be the best form of communication with relatives in this study. I, as researcher was able to interpret the body language and expressions as well as the dialogue of the relatives enabling me to discern as much as possible what relatives were feeling and trying to express to me after the death of their relative.

In the process of assessing and analyzing the data, the recording of the interviews assisted greatly, allowing me to play and replay repeatedly voices and perceive the varied intonations, expressions and subtleties of the interviewee. In this repetition I obtained different levels of meaning to the expressions in each interview which provided greater depth to the subsequent analysis.

With 20 families included in this study, the importance of a single interview for each cannot be overemphasized in terms of its wealth of individual experience and knowledge in revealing something new about the human condition. An experience that can be harnessed for the future in revealing new ways of improving the standards of care, both lay and professional, for each dying person and their families.

Sensitivity to the needs of relatives and patients involved in the study was of paramount importance. As the researcher I provided comprehensive information to patients and relatives on the details of the study. I was a constant active empathetic listener and was present to the patients before death and their relatives ensuring that their needs were fulfilled. Giving comfort and reassurance was also a primary responsibility for me so that patients and relatives felt secure and at ease with their role in the study.

It was obvious from the beginning of this research how essential it was that counseling be available and offered to patients and their families as the need arose and continual contact was maintained between the social worker and myself as the researcher if any relative or dying patient appeared to need counseling.

From my experience as a palliative medicine researcher, I can concur with Bingley, Thomas & Brown, (2008), that we have as palliative medicine clinicians and researchers the opportunity to build on a wide range of narrative research methods with potential to inform and improve healthcare policy, medical and health sciences training and practice, now and in the future. This qualitative enquiry into the moment of death, will be of consequential clinical guidance not only to myself but to other professionals, helping to inform and illuminate, revealing to us more ways and new or recalled old ways of therapeutic management, contributing to the future understanding and treatment of dying patients and their grieving relatives.

Palliative care is a crucial public health issue because everyone will die at some stage. It is well to know what dying can be like. Professionals who work in Palliative care may not necessarily witness the dying process. Yet death is what we are preparing patients to face. This study describes dying and death. We cannot hear the stories of the dead. We can try to hear the stories of the living who have witnessed dying. These relatives care deeply for the individual who is dying. They observe every detail, attending to their role and observing the role of others. They are valuable witnesses.

According to Byock (2002) we know very little about the experience of death, yet death is central to the meaning and value of human life and communities and even though "one can no more look steadily at death than at the sun" (Feifel, 1959), we can at least attempt to unravel its hidden mysteries. Love affirms life in the face of death Byock (2002). This is confirmed as exemplified by this study on the moment of death in a Specialist Palliative Care Unit. Even though Donnelly (1999 (a)) states that there is a danger as carers in our expertise and professionalism of disempowering the dying person and their natural carers, of sidelining the foundation of their relationship, that is love, this study shows that love is profound, demonstrated through service by the carers both lay and professional in the care of the dying and their relatives.

Though Byock (2002) does not explicitly define the meaning of love, in my own understanding of love, as expressed in this study, it is the attentive care to the wellbeing of the patient and relatives by carers and staff, expressed through compassion, dignity, affection, concern, tenderness, words of encouragement and consolation and the direct care of the physical, emotional, psychological and spiritual needs of both patients and their relatives. When love is defined in these terms it is true to say that in this enquiry, love is the cornerstone in the care of the dying. Expressed below are simple gestures, demonstrating loving care given by staff and profoundly appreciated by family members:

"One day I walked onto the ward and a domestic lady cleaning the floor said a big "Hello" to my aunt [lying in the bed] and went over and gave her a big hug. I have never seen that before in any hospital and it touched me very much."

"Before Nora passed away, the nurses were in, changed her nightdress, combed her hair and fixed her up. It was all done with dignity; it was dignity right to the very end."

"The nurses were marvelous to her, marvelous to her, as if there was no one else in the hospital. She got every attention, you couldn't get more. It was a very happy death."

"[There was] total respect of the person."

There is no reason – in present-day law or in ethics – to prevent care from being tender and loving (Byock, 2002). We as professionals need to care for the dying in a manner that treats them as one would treat an honored guest. We can never learn enough from the dying, from those whom we interview and all whom we meet in our research. To them we owe our thanks. The dying patients and those who witness dying are our teachers As Spradley (1979) so succinctly puts it:

"I want to know, what you know in the way you know it. I want to understand the meaning of your experience, to walk in your shoes, to feel things as you feel them, to explain things as you explain them. Will you become my teacher and help me understand ....?"

Appendices

Appendix 8.1
Ethics Letter

Appendix 8.2
Explanation of the study to patients and their families I am conducting research at the Palliative Medicine Unit, with the aim of improving the care of patients and their families and friends. This project involves unobtrusive observation by me, as researcher, recording my impressions, noting conversations and later interviewing sensitively family members and carers. I would be most grateful if you were willing to participate. You may withdraw at any time. I am a researcher and a qualified doctor and am keenly aware that this is a difficult time for you. I believe that the results of this study will benefit others. Your participation and your experience and insight will assist the study greatly.

Researcher: Dr Cliodhna Donnelly

Supervisor: Dr Sinead Donnelly

Appendix 8.3
Consent form used for interview in this study:

I (name) agree to the recording of this interview about the moment of death. I understand the recording and/ or transcript may be used for education purposes, through oral presentation or publication.

Recordings will be safely stored in the research office. A copy of the tape or transcript will be made available to you. You will not be referred to by name in the written transcript or in any report of the results of this enquiry. Your comments on the transcript and the report of this enquiry will be elicited. You are free to withdraw at any time from participation in this enquiry. The form is to be signed by

Interviewee ....

Interviewer ....

Date ....

Appendix 8.4

Questions asked at family interviews:

How are you since n........ died?

What did you find of comfort while n....... was in the Palliative Care Unit?

Do you think n....... was comfortable when he/she died?

Was there anything that could have been improved in n......'s care while he/she was in the Palliative Care Unit?

Can you describe what exactly happened at the time of n......'s death. (Included in this question were: Describe how you felt?

What were your thoughts? Were there any rituals or prayers. If so describe them. Who was present? How many people were there? What was done? What was said?)

What do you think happens to a person when they die? (This question was included in order to reflect on the families attitude towards death and dying which would influence their perception of their relatives death.)

Is there anything else you would like to add

Appendix 8.5
Demographics of Patients included in study

(Select) References

AAHPM (American Academy of Hospice and Palliative Medicine) Position Statement on Palliative Care Research Ethics, 2007. [online] http://www.aahpm.org/positions/researchethics

Addington-Hall J. McPherson C.
"After-Death Interviews with Surrogates/ Bereaved Family Members: Some issues of Validity" in J. Pain Symptom Manage 2001; 22:3:784-91.

Ahmedzai S, Morton A, Reid J, Stevenson R. "Quality of death from lung cancer (patients' reports and relatives' retrospective opinions." in: Watson M, Greer S, Thomas C. (eds.) Psychosocial Oncology; Oxford: Pergamon Press, 1988. (pp 187-192).

Aries P. The Hour of our Death; H. Weaver (Trans.) Hammondsworth: Penguin, 1981.

Aries P. Western attitudes towards death: From the Middleages to the Present. Baltimore: Johns Hopkins University Press, 1974.

Atkinson A. "Kundera's Immortality: The Interview Society and the invention of self." in Qualitative Inquiry 1997;3:304- 25.

Avis M. Incorporating Patients Voices in the Audit Process. Qual. in Health Care 1997: 6:86-91.

Bachelor Report, 200 -
http://www.forpeaceofmind.com.au/Vol2/bachelor report

Baddley A. Human Memory: Theory and Practice; London: Lawrence Erlbaum Associates, 1990.

Banister P., Burman E, Parker I. Qualitative Methods in Psychology: A Research Guide; Buckingham: Open University Press, 1994.

Baumann Z. Postmodern Ethics; Oxford: Blackwell, 1993.

Bell, R. Our People Die Well: Deathbed Scenes in John Wesley's Arminian Magazine in: Mortality 2005; 10:3:210-23.

Berger J.T., Rosner F, Potash J. Communication in Caring for the Terminally-Ill Patients in: J. Palliat. Med. 2000; 3:1:69-73.

Bingley A, Thomas C, Brown J. "Illness Narratives: Developing narrative research in supportive and palliative care: the focus on illness narratives." in: Palliat Med 2008; 22:653-58.

Bingley A, Mc Dermott E, Thomas C, Reeve J, Payne S. "Making sense of dying: a review of narratives written since 1950 by people facing death from cancer and other diseases." Palliat. Med 2006; 20:83-95.

Black N. "Why we need qualitative research" in: J Epidemiol Comm Health 1994; 48:425-6.

Bowling A. "The hospitalization of death: should more people die at home?"
J Med Ethics 1983; 9:158-61.

Bradburn D.Response Effects. In: Rossi P, Wright A, Anderson A. (eds.) Handbook of Survey Research; New York: Academic Press, 1983.

Bradely C. Qualitative vs Quantitative Research Methods; In: Research Methods in Primary Care; Ratcliffe: Oxford, 1997.

Brody H. "Philosophic approaches." In: Crabtree B, Miller W. (eds) Doing Qualitative Research; CA, Sage Publications, 1992. (pp174-85)

Burgess R. "The Medicalization of Dying" in: J Med Philos 1993; 18:269-79.

Byock I. "The Meaning and Value of Death." in: J Palliat Med 2002;5:2:279-88.

Callahan D. The Troubled Dream of Life: In Search of a Peaceful Death;
Touchstone: Simon & Schuster, New York, 1993.

Cancer Institute New South Wales. NSW Cancer Plan, 2004- 2006. http://www.cancerintitutionnewsouthwalesagency/

http://en.wikipedia.org/wiki/nswgovernmentshop/1stnswcancerplan

Cartwright A, Seale C. The natural history f survey (An account of the methodological issues encountered in a study of life before death.) London: King's Fund, 1990.

Cassaret D. "Are Hospices Ready to Participate in Palliative Care Research?" Results of a National Survey. In: J Palliat Med 2002; 5:3:397.

Cassaret DJ, Karlawish JH. Are special ethical guidelines needed for palliative care research? J Pain Symp Manage 2000; 20:130-9.

Charon R. "Narrative Medicine: Form, function and Ethics" in: Ann Int Med 2001; 134:1:83-87.

Chochinov H.M. "Dying, Dignity and New Horizons in Palliative End-of-Life Care." in: CA Cancer J Clin 2006; 56:84- 103.

Chochinov H.M., Cann B. "Interventions to Enhance the Spiritual Aspects of Dying." in: J Palliat Med 2005;8:1:103-15.

Chochinov H.M. "The Culture of Research in Palliative Care: You Probably Think This Song Is About You" in: J Palliat Med 2009; 12:3:215-217.

Clark D. (ed) The Future of Palliative Care; Buckingham: The Open University Press, 1990.

Clark D. "Between hope and acceptance: the medicalisation of dying." in: BMJ, 2002; 324:905-07.

Clark D. What is qualitative research and what can it contribute to palliative care? Palliat Med 1997;11:159-166.

Clark L, Leedy S, McDonald L, Muller B, Lamb C, Mendez T, Kim S, Schowetter R. "Spirituality and Job Satisfaction among Hospice Interdisciplinary Team Members" in: J Pall Med 2007; 10:6:1321-27.

Corr C. Death and Dying, Life and Living; Pacific Grove: Brooks Cole Publishing Company, 1994.

Crabtree B, Miller W. Doing Qualitative Research; Sage, London, 1992

Cressy D. Birth, marriage and death: Ritual religion and the life cycle in Tudor and Stuart England; Oxford:Oxford University Press, 1997.
CSO. Central Statistics Office, 2003. [online]
http://www.cso.ie

Denzin N, Lincoln Y. (eds.) Handbook of Qualitative Research; London: Sage Publications, 1994.

DeRaeve L. "Ethical issues in palliative care research." in: Palliat Med 1994; 8 :298-305

Dey I. Creating Categories: Qualitative Data Analysis; London: Routledge, 1993. (pp 94-112)

Dingwall R. "Accounts, interviews and observations." In: Miller G, Dingwall R. (eds) Context and Method in Qualitative Research; Thousand Oaks, CA: Sage Publications, 1997.

Donnelly S. Symptoms and Quality of Life in Patients with Advanced Cancer.
Doctorate of Medicine by Thesis (MD), NUI Library, Galway, 1995.

Donnelly S. [Personal communication] 2008.

Donnelly S.(a) "Folklore associated with dying in the West of Ireland." in: Palliat Med 1999;13:57-62.

Donnelly S.(b) "Traditions Associated with Dying in the West of Scotland." in: J Palliat Care 1999; 15:4:64-69.

Donnelly S, Battley J.(b) Relatives' experience of the moment of death in a tertiary referral hospital, 2009. [in print]

Donnelly S, Michael N, Donnelly C. "Experience of the moment of death at home" in: Mortality 2006; 11:4:352-67.

Donnelly S, Donnelly C. (a) "The Experience of the Moment of Death in a Specialist Palliative Care Unit." in: IMJ 2009; 102:5:143-49.

Doyle D, Hanks G, McDonald N. (eds.) Oxford Textbook of Palliative Medicine, 1st ed.; Oxford Med. Publications, 1993.

Doyle D, Hanks G, Mc Donald N. (eds.) Oxford Textbook of Palliative Medicine; 2nd Edition; Oxford Med Publications, 1998.

Dunlop R, Davies R, Hockley J.M. "Preferred versus actual place of death; hospital palliative care support team experience." in: Palliat Med 1989; 3:3:197-01

Dye J, Shatz I, Rosenburg B, Coleman S. "Constant Comparative Method: A Kaleidescope of Data." in: The Qualitative Report 2000;4:1/2

Dyer K .In Search of a Definition of a Good Death, 2006. [online] http://dying.about.com/od/palliativeendoflifecare

Ellershaw J, Ward C. "Care of the dying patient: the last hours or days of life." in: BMJ 2003;326:30-34.

Feifel H. (ed) The Meaning of Death; McGraw Hill: New York, 1959. (pp 11)

Feinberg AW. "The Care of Dying Patients." in: Ann Int Med 1997; 126:2:164-165.

Field D, Douglas C, Jagger C. "Terminal Illness: views of patients and their lay carers." in: Palliat Med 1995; 9:45-54.

Field M, Cassel CK. Approaching death: Improving Care at the End of Life; Washington DC: National Academic Press; 1997.

Fleck F. WHO wants more palliative care for Europeans. BMJ 2004;329:248.

Fontana A, Frey J. "Interviewing: the art of science." in: Denzin NK, Lincoln YS, (eds).

Collecting and interpreting Qualitative Materials; Sage, Thousand Oaks, 1998.

Fontana A. "Postmodern trends in interviewing." in: Gubrum J, Holstein J. (eds.)
Handbook of Qualitative Research, Context and Method; Thousand Oaks, CA: Sage Publications, 2002. (pp. 161-75)

Fontana A, Frey J. "The Interview." in: Denzin N, Lincoln Y (eds.) Sage Handbook of Qualitative Research; 3rd Edition, Sage Publications, 2005.

Frankl V. Man's Search for Meaning; New York: Simon & Schuster, 1984. (pp135)

Fried T, van Doorn C, O' Leary J, Tinnetti M, Drickamer M. "Older Persons Preferences for Site of Terminal Care." in: Ann Int Med 1999; 131:2: 109-12.

Gallup GH. The George H. Gallup International Institute: Spiritual beliefs and the dying process: A report on a national survey, conducted by the Nathan Cummings Foundation and the Fezter Institute, 1997. [online] –
http://www.ncf.org/reports/rptfetzercontents

About The Authors

Dr. Clíodhna Donnelly is a qualified medical practitioner. In 1997 she was conferred with a Masters Degree in Public Health Medicine from University College Dublin (UCD). Subsequent to this she worked in various positions including as Area Medical Officer for the North-West Donegal Region of Ireland. During the year 2000 she worked as a Research Registrar in Palliative Medicine at Milford Care Centre, Limerick. The research on the "Moment of Death" study was funded by the South Western Health Board. She was conferred with her Medical Doctorate in December 2010 at University College Dublin (UCD).

Dr. Mícheál Ó hAodha currently works at the University of Limerick. He has written and edited many books in both Irish and English as relating to Irish oral history and culture and the stories of the Irish diaspora including: American "Outsider": Stories from the Irish Traveller Diaspora. (2007) (with T.J. Vernon); "The Turn of the Hand": A Memoir from the Irish Margins (with Mary Warde) (2010); "Insubordinate Irish": Travellers in the Text; Manchester: MUP (2011), Slán le hÉirinn; BÁC: Coiscéim (2012).

Printed in Great Britain
by Amazon

57246874R00099